The Tangled Mane

The Tangled Mane

The Lions Tour to Australia, 2001

Eddie Butler

BLOOMSBURY

First Published in Great Britain 2001

Copyright © 2001 by Eddie Butler

The moral right of the author has been asserted

All photographs, including the front cover © Empics,
except for page 2 of the plate section © Action Images and
page 7 bottom © Action Images

Bloomsbury Publishing Plc, 38 Soho Square, London W1V 3HB

A CIP catalogue record for this book
is available from the British Library

ISBN 0 7475 5741 1

10 9 8 7 6 5 4 3 2 1

Typeset by Hewer Text Ltd, Edinburgh
Printed in Great Britain by Clays Ltd, St Ives plc

Contents

1

To begin at the end with bits from the middle

A line-out probably does not count among the most advanced of human activities. A catch and drive at the front probably won't contribute a whole lot to the conquest of space. When you ponder the line-out, you might be tempted to ask just a single question. Why?

But it has its place. And on a warm, damp night on the second Saturday of July in 2001, two groups of rugby players took up their positions in Stadium Australia, Sydney, and prepared to engage in the strange ritual. Fourteen forwards, who understood the ways of the line-out and who knew whether to boost, block or jump, stood in two rows, the one distant from the other by the length of your average right jab. One hooker stood on the touchline, bending his head to hear a shout, the coded signal that would tell him where to throw the ball he was trying to rub dry. His opposite number stood a yard away, staring at him.

Dear All,
Secret letter out of the Gulag. Read this, then eat it.
   This is a nightmare. The boys are treated like children. Train, train, train. Meeting, meeting, meeting. There's no end to it. If we'd known it was going to be like this, we'd never have come . . .

Two scrum halves stood shouting at their forwards. Twelve backs, who remained immune to the charms of the ritual, stretched across the field in two lines, twenty metres apart. The three-quarters were staring towards the ends of the pitch. Behind the posts and high into the night sky were stacked row upon row of red shirts. The forwards faced the touchline. Before them was a cliff-face of green, gold and yellow. Heaving chests on the field of play; held breath in the stands. Thirty players and 84,188 spectators.

> Dear outside world,
> It's me again. The mutineers met again tonight. Broke curfew and slipped out. If one of us cracked, we'd all crack. Some of the lads have said they'd leave right now. The guards stole our Red Cross parcels today . . .

The tryline was the stretch of a telescopic second row away. It was defended by Australia. The Lions of Britain and Ireland were attacking and would throw the ball into the line-out. They had to score. On one throw, on one catch, and on one drive lay the fortunes of their entire tour. At stake were the Test and the series against the world champions. On this throw would come either victory, with showers of praise and riches, or defeat that would deliver only a can-opener. Wealth or worms awaited.

Keith Wood of Ireland, bald and world-class, checked the signal again and wiped the ball one last time. Martin Johnson of England, the Lions' captain, the totem, the brooding giant, braced himself. The hooker drew back the ball . . .

> Dear anybody out there,
> Couldn't give a monkey's. HMS *Miserable* sails on . . .

This is the story of a rugby union tour. It was without doubt the weirdest and most controversial travelling circus in the history of a most peculiar game.

2

Further back in time

I found myself looking forward to six weeks in Australia by looking back on three days in France. This, incidentally, should give no cause for alarm. Strange avenues are commonplace in rugby. In fact, drifting on the irrational is as compulsory as tackling practice. And since there was to be more than enough of that particular delight on the Lions tour of 2001, odd diversions are inevitable.

It was about twelve years ago that a grandly titled colloquium was held in Toulon. If the title was grand, the subject matter was earthy. The seminar in this city where Cote d'Azur chic meets naval port brutish was dedicated to 'Violence in Sport', and was an attempt by the Municipality to purge the collective Provençal conscience after the death of a rugby player from nearby Marseilles in a third-division match.

No finger was ever pointed, but the victim had basically been kicked to death at the bottom of a ruck. Now, this had nothing to do with the Lions. Or at least it had nothing to do with preparations for the tour of 2001, which at this stage were being conducted along strictly wholesome lines. But the question of fighting was bound to arise at some stage over the six weeks. It went with the territory. And Australia was one vast territory, which contained a whole mine of memories of the last time the Lions had paid a visit.

The Lions of 1989 had done little to endear themselves to their hosts. Winning the series hadn't helped, but it went beyond that. This had been the first occasion when the best players of England, Ireland, Scotland and Wales combined to go on tour exclusively to Australia, and these pioneers had increasingly earned themselves a reputation for tactics beyond the pale.

Having lost the first Test, the Lions came back to take the series 2–1. It had not been pretty. Most of the unsavoury incidents were confined in time-honoured fashion to the forwards, but when scrum half Robert Jones stood on the foot of his opposite number, Nick Farr-Jones, at the first scrum in the second Test, and sparked a mini-riot, it was clear that even the smallest of tourists had been intoxicated by the desire to terrorise the Wallabies.

The Lions tour of 1989 and the Toulon colloquium may have embraced – or tackled, as the parlance would have it – the same thorny issue, but no, it wasn't that overall theme of violence that had triggered memories. Rather, it was some professor from Paris talking about jousting.

In lecture theatres across Toulon there had been biochemists talking about this flush of hormones here and that surge of particle energy there; there had been an in-depth analysis of the ways of the masters of disorder at that time, 'les hooligans anglais' in the world of football. But it was the prof and his jousting that came back to me.

It was to do with that old line by George Orwell, the one about sport being war without the shooting. The professor said that in the time before sport, competitive instincts tended to manifest themselves as war with the shooting. In the absence of the vehicles of containment – gloves, padding, laws, rules, referees, handicaps – people who were what we now call 'pumped up' took all too readily to the real battleground. And before a king or emperor knew it, half the homeland's finest warriors and workers had turned into a pile of corpses or were limping away missing a limb or two.

Somebody thought it might be preferable to encourage the Mongol hordesmen or Assyrian noblemen, or whomever, to let off steam without actually paying the ultimate price for finishing as runner-up. Hence, horse races that ended at a finish line rather than with a wade into the enemy's lines; hence, the joust with blunted lance. Hence, sport, said the prof.

And it just struck me that if ever modern sport had slipped back a few millennia to those guinea-pig days of the barest of safeguards it was now. It was as if Genghis Khan had yielded to political correctness and decreed that nobody out of battle-ground office hours should actually be, you know, slaughtered. On the other hand, it might be mildly engaging to put on a spectacle that reminded everyone that it was only last week that the lads were laying waste to half of Asia Minor.

So, it was showtime. The Rugby World Cup, the Five/Six Nations and the Tri Nations had all had their moments, but seldom had rugby offered such a promise of sustained, unrestrained rivalry as the Lions tour of 2001, an odyssey to the home of the world champions, Australia. The rugby of the Old World was on a high, triggered by a revolution in England, of all places. Power had shifted from the most uptight, conservative bastion of reaction to a new order. A last-gasp revolt of the Luddite amateurs had been put down by proxy vote at a Special General Meeting. After six long years of chaos in the governance of rugby in England, professionalism at last had the chance to become a working system. As if by way of celebration, Leicester and Harlequins had become respectively the Cup and Shield club champions of Europe.

Above the clubs, the national team had finally emerged from its chrysalis to rewrite the way rugby was played in the northern hemisphere. Clive Woodward's Team England had sometimes appeared to be in mothballs, rather than metamorphosis, but now his players had seen his vision and had zealously taken to his game of athleticism, speed and width. Other countries were rushing now to find a response. Scotland and Wales, desperate not to let their giant neighbour speed off without them, were buzzing with new ideas. New franchises, new approaches, new structures were all the talk.

In Ireland there was a greater confidence in the way the pro game had been handled since it was dropped on the unsuspecting amateur world in 1995. The Irish were more measured in their response to England's excellence. After all, they were unbeaten themselves in the Six Nations, having won against Italy away and France at home. But Ireland's challenge to England had been disrupted by the foot and mouth crisis. International rugby in general, between February and the departure of the Lions for Australia on 1 June, was thrown into limbo by the plague. The Six Nations for once had failed to satisfy the demand for drama. Because of the postponements there could be no English Grand Slam. Nor conversely could there be a Triple Crown of upsets, whereby Ireland became the third country in successive years, after Wales and Scotland, to deny England the top prize in the European game. Unresolved lay the Six Nations. Ireland's three remaining matches, against Scotland, Wales and most of all England, who were unbeaten after four rounds, would not be played until the autumn. This provoked, strangely enough, no wilting of interest in what was to come. If anything, the Lions became more compelling. There was more space to fill with tour speculation, more time to dwell on the summer ahead. Less rugby meant more contention. Would the Irish suffer in selection now that the selectors had not seen them play?

And all the while, Australia patiently waited. All that could be heard were mutual messages of admiration passing back and forth between Rod Macqueen and Graham Henry. They used to cross swords as respective coaches of the ACT Brumbies and the Auckland Blues in the early years of the Super 12 competition in the southern hemisphere; now they were to come face to face as the coaches of the two most powerful Test outfits in the world.

Australia used to provide but a warm-up for Lions teams that were on their way to New Zealand. The Wallabies were re-nowned for playing a style of rugby that was pleasing to the eye. Sometimes they were successful, more often not. In the 1980s they suddenly rose to become a power in their own right. An inspirational Schools team from the late 1970s stayed together and blossomed in adulthood around outside half Mark Ella. In 1984 he orchestrated their moves as they completed a Grand Slam tour of the Home Unions. They were every bit as revolutionary then as England were to become in the new millennium. Ella couldn't kick very well; so, he ran and passed his way into the annals as one of the all-time greats.

In a way, however, that first wave of the eighties never really crashed upon the shore. In the first World Cup of 1987 the Wallabies lost to France. At home, at that. The semi-final may have been one of the most gripping Tests ever, with another all-time great, France's fullback Serge Blanco, scoring a last-gasp try to steal the game, but to Australia that meant nothing. They had underachieved.

In 1989 they lost at home again, to the Lions. David Campese, magician, entertainer and the most prolific try-scorer in the history of the game, gifted the Lions a try in the third Test, a decider more notable for its haymakers than its sleight of hand. Praise for the Lions from Australian quarters was grudgingly given.

It all came good for Australia and for Campese in the 1990s. They stuck largely to a dazzling style and won the second World Cup in 1991 by beating England in the final at Twickenham. Only to lose to them again in 1995 in the third World Cup in South Africa. A drop goal in the quarter-final by Rob Andrew fuelled the saga of punch and counter-punch between the two countries.

In 1999 Australia won their second World Cup, at Cardiff's Millennium Stadium. They alone had won the Webb Ellis Cup twice. England had never won it. Nobody from Europe ever had. After victory in 1999 the Australians carried on winning. They beat New Zealand and South Africa to take the Tri Nations title in 2000. There was a slight difference now. Under Rod Macqueen they played a much harder-nosed brand of rugby. No improvisation now by the likes of Campese, that might win or lose Test matches. The Wallabies were drilled into a mean beast of a machine that kept and kept possession of the ball. They were programmed to know exactly what to do in every position on the field. They boasted the best defence in the game and the best fitness levels. Now Rod Macqueen's proven performers were to come up against the hastily assembled ensemble of English, Irish,

Scottish and Welsh, coached by a New Zealander, Graham
Henry. A motley crew? Maybe, but they came from a corner
of rugby's empire that was seething with notions of progress and
adventure.

For Macqueen this was his last throw. The fifty-one-year-old
had already announced that he would be standing down after
the Tri Nations series that would follow the Lions series. Beating
the Lions was all he had left to achieve. He had a business to run.
He'd had treatment a few years earlier for a brain tumour. There
was a quieter life to look forward to.

For Graham Henry this was a first. Three years previously he
had arrived in Wales with no experience of rugby at international level, and now he was in charge of the best that Europe
could offer. Two emperors were about to send out their knights.
And they were merely at the head of the expeditionary force. If
the Lions of 2001 deserved a place in history it was because they
inspired a movement. Behind came camp-followers by the
thousand, by the tens of thousand. They would grow by the
day into a moving manifestation of unconditional support.

They provoked wide-eyed amazement among the local population. Australia was mobilised to counter this invasion. It
became a clash of colour and clamour, red against green and
gold, of ballad against ballad, 'Waltzing Matilda' against
'Waltzing O'Driscoll'. On the field the clashes grew brutal as
the Test series approached. Tight units were formed, specialist
skirmishers, experts at giving more than they took. And as
solidarity grew there, tales of mutiny circulated. And all the
while the standard of rugby was stretching upwards, way off the
scale.

Nothing like this had ever been seen before. The professor of
history in Toulon might have to reconsider his theory of sport as
the art of keeping the warrior in one piece.

3

Back to the start

Where did it all begin? Did we have to go back all the way to a time near the end of the last millennium, to the compilation of the very first long-list of candidates and the drafting of a rough itinerary in Australia? Presumably it was Syd Millar, chairman of the Lions committee, who one day coughed and called a metting to order. And started a debate as to whether so-and-so's propensity to drift out of alignment on the blind side might one day in June 2001 be a liability, or whether the beds in Coffs Harbour were long enough.

But to delve too far back into the history of a Lions tour is to give the process a length that undermines the frenzy of moulding players from four different countries into one team capable of taking on the world champions on their home soil. The sense of working in condensed time and space would hardly be enhanced by a vote of thanks for all those selectors and advisers whose efforts over the preceding months had made the venture possible. It's rude to leave people out, but romance in sport is not made by everything going according to meticulous plans laid months in advance.

So, for the sake of drama, the starting date for the Lions tour of 2001 shall be given here as Wednesday, 25 April of the same year, five weeks and two days before the party left for Perth, Western Australia. That was the day when the names of the thirty-seven players and thirteen members of the management were announced.

It was hardly a date heralded by fanfare and pomp. Hotels at Heathrow Airport did not come with much more than the whiff of aviation fuel and triple-glazing. But the Crown Plaza was at least a foretaste of touring. It at least smacked of haste and purpose. No-nonsense stopovers and then off again.

Martin Johnson was to be the captain. The meanest hombre in the Midlands was to lead the Lions as he led his club, Leicester and his country, England. There would be no blarney. He described himself in the Media Guide as 'very dull'. Same Guide: How do you prepare for a big rugby match? Get changed into my rugby kit. He wasn't dull at all. But he'd be damned if he was going to give anything away. His secrets would be kept under lock and key, like a dowager duchess's diamonds in her safety-deposit box at the bank where the captain still did some part-time work.

There had been some speculation that Keith Wood of Ireland might be given the captaincy. He was more engaging in public. He too was captain of his country. Martin's track record was longer. He'd been a foot-soldier on the tour to New Zealand in 1993, a replacement who went straight into the Test team. The Lions lost that series 1–2. On the next tour, to South Africa in 1997, he was the captain, and the Lions won 2–1. Experience, not affability, was the priority. With England Martin had shown that he could be progressive, espousing a style that revolutionised European rugby. He had even led a strike, but warming his hands over the brazier at an England picket-line spoke of the very solidarity that would be sought on the tour of Australia.

Woody, who'd played under Martin in South Africa, also had a bit of a personal history of heresy. The issue was the same: impatience at the governing bodies' inability to implement change off the field as quickly as they, the players had moved the game forward on it. But the Irishman's strike was a one-man walkout. A free-thinker. This was no time for taking a gamble.

Would there be any risks taken at all? Simon Taylor, the twenty-one-year-old Scottish back-row forward with just four caps to his name, was the one surprise selection. The surprise omissions? Scott Gibbs, the Welsh centre who had been exactly that, a central figure, on the previous two Lions tours, to New Zealand in 1993 and South Africa in 1997. And Gregor Townsend of Scotland, who had been inside Scott in South Africa. Both were overlooked, although the make-up of the squad of thirty-seven failed to incite any real grievances. It was a question of form at the time.

The party was loaded with English players, eighteen of them, a figure that might at one time have had the Celts growling; but even rugby union, with its rich tribal feuds, could now appreciate a good team when it saw one.

Tours packed with representatives of one particular country, like the Lions of 1977, who were preponderantly Welsh, had not succeeded in the past. But clinical assessment of ability in the professional age came before satisfying some racial quota. England had eighteen because that was how many fitted the bill of athletic ability allied with mental fortitude. End of argument for the moment, although the whole question of strength of mind would be revisited many times before the planes left Australia to bring the party home again.

Ireland might have raised an eyebrow at having only six representatives, but they didn't because Ireland were the best tourists on the planet, and good tourists couldn't really start slagging off their team-mates before they had even met for the first time. Wales had ten, and Scotland three. The Scots really would have liked to have a grumble at that. What, three? But they didn't, probably because three didn't form a very noisy quorum of victimisation. Wales kept quiet. Graham Henry was their coach.

This press conference was to set a trend that would become all too familiar as the weeks passed. Nothing could start without the sponsors' billboard being ready. Players in Manly in weeks to come would stand around while 'Land' and 'Rover' were jigsawed together behind them. Here at least the board was up and shining as the tour manager, Donal Lenihan, welcomed everybody and apologised for the slight delay. This, too, would change along the way, as slight delay became long delay.

Punctuality was to melt into a word from a foreign language. But here on day one it mattered not. Donal said how proud everyone was to play for the Lions. 'The Lions are special,' was launched as the mantra. The coach, Graham Henry, said that yes, of course, they had a plan to beat the Wallabies, but no, he wasn't going to tell anyone what it was.

The secrecy was based on the fact that this was the shortest Lions tour ever. Ten matches in six weeks, including three Tests at the far end. Before the first of these, they only had six games, two of which were going to be warm-up acts, missionary work in far-flung places. The last midweek game before the opening Test was going to be a dirt-track special. The Lions had to know their Test team before then. In short, they had just three hard matches in which to select their best squad of twenty-two, fine-tune it and bring it up to the speed of the world champions. Everything was on a condensed scale.

They could have made a drama out of this. This was a breathless race against time. But they didn't. This inaugural Lions occasion, played out to an assembly of media representatives large enough to overbook one of the Jumbos rumbling past nearby, was as prosaic as a list of names that do not rhyme. But it still carried that sense of mission launched, of an adventure underway, if only because of the roll-call of destinations for which the chosen players were bound: the Gabba and Ballymore in Brisbane, the WACA in Perth, Colonial Stadium, Melbourne and Stadium Australia itself in Sydney. Not forgetting, of course, Dairy Farmers Stadium and North Power Stadium in Townsville and Gosford respectively.

It was non-stop geographical poetry from that moment on. Like Stockport. Eight days later I went there to see Martin Johnson. He was at the adidas (sic) factory in Pepper Road for the launch of the tourists' playing strip, a 'climalite' shirt, light of weight, heavy on durability, absorbent, hard to grip in the tackle and yet responsive to the touch of the line-out booster. It had the stamp of space-age technology all over it. With its grandad collar, it had fashion accessory writ even larger. The supporters at home and the travelling circus would purchase each and every single one of the 250,000 replica shirts before the tour was a week old.

Martin Johnson, a rugby player of massive stature, was here in a clothing factory because that's what Lions captains were expected to do. But, like Henry at Heathrow, the skipper in Stockport was giving little away. Apart from his features, that is. The second-row forward was gigantically photogenic, with ledges and eyebrows under his brow as craggy and shaggy as the most remote corners of the Forest of Dean. Johnson was no disciple of romance. He talked of advancement only through hard work, or the sheer toil of progress. England, his England, had not exploded to the top of the European game by dint of some flash of light and the sudden gift of creativity. Rather, they had trained their nuts off, so that in the heat of the action, when they and their opponents were too exhausted to do anything other than to draw in their next breath, the instinct to keep the game fluid would function automatically. In the eternal quest for the triumph of sentimentality in rugby, you might not be best advised to keep a space for a final thought from the Lions' captain. But always keep a space for him by your side in case of an emergency in a dark alley.

The coach had not had his say; the captain had not had his say. Everything went quiet. Johnson and his Leicester team, including fellow Lions Neil Back and Austin Healey, went off to Paris to win the European Cup in a draining, bruising epic of a final against Stade Français. Keith Wood, Will Greenwood and Jason Leonard played for Harlequins the next day in the European Shield final against Narbonne, a game that was every bit as compelling, percussive and, after extra time, victorious. Graham Henry went off to New Zealand to rest awhile in his homeland rather than stay in Europe and count the collisions.

He returned and the Lions came together six days before leaving for Australia. Tylney Hall in Hampshire was their first hotel and bonding the players was the first public theme. They were given musical instruments and told to form a band, or were ordered up structures that were impossible to climb without teamwork. Laughter up a ladder and discord from the orchestra filled the air.

In their meetings the Lions were expected to give of themselves. They had to stand up as individuals in front of the others and dig a little into their own character: what made them tick, what got up their nose, their weak and their strong points. If it sounded a little like something corporate out of middle-management America, the mission statement was yet to come.

Graham Henry, about to turn fifty-five, said that he was a bit too cynical to be a good cuddler and was happy to leave that to others. The former headmaster of Kelston Boys' High School in Auckland had still played his instrument at the concert and had declared himself the only one in time and tune, but he was probably more at ease in his office working on the aims and goals of the tour.

He'd been the coach of Wales for the past three years, having been enormously successful at sub-test level with the Auckland Blues back home in New Zealand. In the slightly hysterical rugby environment of South Wales he had immediately been given the title of Great Redeemer, and almost as quickly put through a mill of criticism whenever his sides lost to England, as they had for the past two seasons.

There was also Grannygate. This birth-certificate scandal involved players, like Shane Howarth and Brett Sinkinson of New Zealand, who had somehow managed to find a grandparent born in Wales. The grandparents' Kiwi descendants were thereby qualified to play for Wales. And they had. Subsequent research unfortunately revealed that no such qualification existed, and that the players' ancestors were about as Welsh as moussaka. The coach was probably a bit unlucky that the Welsh scam was exposed only as a contiguous finding in a report into players with suspect Scottish qualifications.

Losing to England at home, by lots, had not done much for Henry's Lions cause outside Wales, Scotland and Ireland. In other words, in England. It was not a prerequisite for the Lions coach to be working at international level. Carwyn James had coached the 1971 Lions to victory in New Zealand while coach of Llanelli, and Ian McGeechan in South Africa 1997 had been coach of Northampton. But in 2001 not many names other than those of national team coaches had seriously been put forward. And only England offered a home-grown alternative.

Warren Gatland, the coach of Ireland, was as Kiwi as Graham Henry. Ian McGeechan of Scotland had already turned down the chance to go on a fourth Lions tour. Which left Clive Woodward, the England manager who had masterminded the defeat of the Welsh in the opening fixture of the 2001 Six Nations championship. As with everything to do with Clive, it was never quite clear whether he had allowed his name to go into the hat or not. What was known was that he always said that it had been wrong to appoint an outsider. Graham Henry was already under extra pressure to succeed.

He was a small man, and was desert-dry with his one-liners. But right now at Tylney Hall he was working on a longer script, something more grandiose, more earnest. The Lions' mission, he drummed into the players, was to become the best there had ever been in order to beat the best. The work would be hard but there was to be a balance between work and play. There was fun to be had along the way. Everything hinged on the paramount virtues of respect, honesty, integrity, dignity, responsibility and mutual support. Individually they all had to get along; collectively they had to click almost instantaneously. Fifty hearts had to beat as one.

This was all pretty good speech-day stuff. But it came with a confidentiality clause. Players were required to sign up to a code of conduct. They would be honest and candid with each other within the camp, but that's where it would stay. In-house. No leaks. This Masonic secrecy stood in stark contrast to the very modern phenomenon of mass-media interest in the game. Just about every player was signed up by a newspaper or a television channel, by radio or the Internet to provide the insider's per-spective to the outside world. Good money was being paid for . . . nothing? Keeping your playing secrets from the opposition was one thing, but playing at being a secret society was going to make the tour very frisky. The inclination to reveal nothing was very revealing.

Was anybody paying any notice to the fine sentiments of the mission statement anyway? In the privacy of the training sessions there was already urgency to the work of assistant coach Phil Larder as he laid out his theory of defence. This was no laughing matter. Fifty hearts beating as one? Thirty-seven were pumping furiously. It had taken the ex-rugby league coach years to build his theory of impenetrability and fine-tune England rugby union's mighty version of it. Now he had just days to construct something that would have to be even stronger.

There was so much time for rugby that in this first week there was very little time to socialise. If any. Steve Black, the fitness conditioner – and the 'cuddler' – saw nothing wrong in that. There was an overriding priority at this stage, he would say, to make the players aware of the size of the challenge ahead. Six weeks of tourism and partying did not lie ahead.

Three days before departure the whole squad was wheeled out before the media. It was a day drenched in sunlight in deepest Hampshire and the croquet lawn between the hotel and the lake at the end of the gardens echoed politely to the sound of chit-chat. Henry said he was further ahead with his preparations than he had dared hope. The players said that they had been put through a gruelling mill.

That night they went up by coach to the City of London for a black-tie dinner. This was the new face of the Lions game. Not the black tie, which was an echo of the old days of formal wear and informal revelry. And not really the fund-raising, for the Lions had always been good at flogging complimentary tickets and signed bits of kit for the beer kitty. But this was money-making on a new level. This was taking the Lions brand to the City and flaunting it. Even the one social outing came with its corporate packaging. After a journey of two and a half hours, and to the sound of a live big band, they were clapped into a huge tent on a derelict site on Bishopsgate Viaduct. Two Lions per table; one Lion for every four guests. It was a black-tie banker.

The presentation was slick and the players were dutifully attentive as the speeches came and went and the auctions began.

But you knew that they knew that this event on a boiling-hot evening at the end of May in a tent on a bridge in the City of London was the phoney war at its height. Two days later the sighs of relief were as audible as the roar of the jet engines as they left Heathrow and Hampshire and Hospitality behind them.

4

Flights of fancy

The press were not far behind. A large part of the pack's first wave – about fifteen – was booked on a Thai Airways flight out of Heathrow on the Monday night, three days after the players left, five days before the Derby. I mention horse-racing's Classic only because I happened to spend my last afternoon in England stretched out on Epsom Downs beneath a glorious June sun, watching the planes pass overhead.

There in the sunlight I felt a nostalgic wave. My old coach at Pontypool for the greater part of my playing career had been the one and only Ray Prosser, a shy extrovert, a brutal, gentle soul who could weep great round tears and bellow massive obscenities in the same breath. Before he coached Pontypool out of the doldrums in the 1970s on a diet of – how can I put this? – forward play in its most extreme form, he had been a prop and second row for his beloved home-town club, for Wales and for the 1959 Lions. In fact, it was while on that tour to New Zealand that he had seen his vision of how rugby should be played. Its manifestation was the hard, ruthless and yet strangely poetic pack of Otago. South Island Otago, where they invented and perfected rucking. Where you lay on the ground at your peril. Where shirts were shredded and flesh was flayed.

Transmuting Pontypool into Otago ran into a couple of problems. First, by the time Pross had gone from player to coach and inspired Pontypool's renaissance through the absolute

– some would say dark – arts as enshrined in the Otago doctrine, sensitivities had gone the other way. The game was less tolerant of excess. Our Pontypool of the late 1970s and early eighties was a pariah club. We rather liked such a tag, although we did lose rather a lot of games. Not on the scoreboard necessarily. We were just struck off other clubs' fixture lists.

Second, Pross hated New Zealand. Not for being New Zealand, but because it was a long way from home. Anywhere beyond Cwmbran, five miles south of Pontypool, made him twitchy. The thought of going to the other side of the globe, and by air of all modes of transport, must have terrified him.

He hated flying. But his fear of taking to the air became, when his feet were on the ground, a fascination with the flying machine. He worked in slag-reduction on the dump at the bottom end of Panteg steelworks just outside Pontypool. On hot summer days he would lie out on the warm corrugated-iron roof of his squat tea-brew shelter amidst the mountains of steaming waste from the furnaces and watch the planes go by, on their way to and from America. He could tell Boeings from DC10s on sound alone and could tell you the thrust of each and every engine whose rumble reached down to his ear . . .

How would the Lions of 2001 play? Graham Henry had done some transmuting of his own. He had reprocessed the alignment of the Welsh backs on his arrival from Auckland, asking them to play much flatter than they had previously. With Neil Jenkins distributing passes from outside half it had for a time made opposition teams think twice, although its impact was not quite as mind-boggling as England's subsequent offering of deep interspersed with flat, of pass mixed up with kick. Henry's record with Wales, given the state of play in 1998 and the depth of talent at his disposal, was impressive, but the more he settled into the job the more he seemed to become a cautious coach. Or rather, a cautious selector. Players with bulk and power had usually been given the nod over players with pace and slender physique.

He had, however, taken the gamble of selecting Jason Robinson for his Lions tour. The Manchester Sale wing could be dazzling, but he had had very few opportunities with England, and he was not Johah Lomu. He was hardly slender, being 100 per cent muscle, but he was about a third as big as New Zealand's outsize wing. Henry recognised, however, that the player who had transferred from rugby league could do something special. Jason had a very interesting history. His had been a conversion not so much from league to union as from wild to devout. He had gone from being one who stayed out till late on the streets, to one who went out on to the streets late to offer comfort to the homeless. Now he was very quiet and very determined.

Jason would be the object of much interest in Australia, if only because the public at large there had at least heard of him from his days in league. To have played against Joe Roff or Damian Smith didn't mean that much, but here was a player who'd marked Wendell Sailor. Australia knew who he was. Jason would also soon thrust his name into the public conscience with his ability to leave the very best defenders clutching at air. He could go from a standing start to full pace in half a metre.

But he was short. In size and on experience. It was generally assumed that Dan Luger of Saracens, if ever he could shake off the injuries that had plagued his season – his career – would be the number one winger on tour.

And would the wingers be of any relevance? Defence in the Test series was going to be massively important, as choreographed by two ex-league men, Phil Larder for the Lions and John Muggleton for the Wallabies. And if the defence coaches did not monopolise every minute of training, then the forwards' coaches would. On the Lions side that meant Andy Robinson, the coach of England. He was certainly claiming every second available to him, plus more, as he rushed to perfect the basics. Could there possibly be any time left to work on something wider, something lighter of touch, that would bring the flyers into play?

There I was on Epsom Downs staring up at the planes circling London, not really knowing one from the other, except that soon enough I'd be on board a Thai Jumbo: I quite liked flying. But first came my rendezvous. To go from my home in Monmouthshire to Heathrow via the home of the Derby is a roundabout route, but it had something to do with taking delivery of a video camera, which I was to carry to Australia and give to Neil Jenkins. The highest points-scorer in the history of Test rugby was going to keep a video diary of his tour.

That seemed simple enough. But not long afterwards I found myself at the airport check-in desk. I was shaking my head before the routine question about sir being asked to carry items of luggage not belonging to sir. I thought that if I tried to explain that on Epsom Downs I had been given a camera by a freelance producer who was en route from Dublin to São Paolo, I might be not so much bound for Australia as in shackles before Special Branch.

Soon, however, we were safely on our way. And soon I was off down old nostalgia avenue again. There was something about that day. Perhaps it was the trance of long-haul flight, or perhaps it was the first of the pork curries at 41,000 feet, but soon I was drifting back . . .

I went on my first Lions tour, as a player of all things, in 1983. Please bear with me, for I'd only been on three and they came at landmark intervals for me, roughly ten years apart.

The tour of 1983 broke all records for being the worst – by far – in the long history of Lions tours. Not to be an original selection was not a compliment, although we, the also-rans, were spared a lot of the pain of being kicked from one end of New Zealand to the other. Also, anyone left at home had a fair chance of being called out as a replacement. There was a lot of ferrying to and fro that summer. Out went the able-bodied; back came the crocked. Anyone who had ever worn boots was told to keep fit.

In a way, that was easy. Wales went on tour that summer to Spain. Without our Lions we were called Wales B, but it was still half the full Welsh team. It was good missionary stuff. We were the first team to play against the Basque Country in the post-

Franco era. It was a touching occasion to see the Basque flag raised and the anthem of Euskadi sung with a fervour that matched Cardiff Arms Park at its most swollen-chested. The locals in Guernica had even spent the entire night clearing away most of the stones that lay on the playing surface. We had nearly spoilt their moment of nationhood by saying that if the stones didn't go, we would.

We opened with an unconvincing victory there, went unbeaten across the Iberian peninsula and finished with a handsome win, if I say so myself, over Spain under the baking-hot midday sun of Madrid. I was captain, and I was very chuffed that I kept my pre-match talk together as manager Rhys Williams time after time hurled his supper of the night before down the toilet on the other side of a very thin wall. Giggling before a Test was not in the manual, although we did play very well at times that day. It was only against Spain, I hear you say, and it was true that we were conscious of the rather more arduous rugby trial taking place on the other side of the world. But we had a good time in that early summer of '83.

Rhys – RH as he had been known ever since his legendary playing days in the second row – had been relaxed and generous as a manager. The only time he was slightly irritated was when he discovered that some of the players had been putting late-night drinks on his room bill. He shared his vexation with John Perkins, a senior player and a club-mate of mine at Pontypool.

The Perk, according to the rota, was duty-boy that day, which meant, in the normal course of life on tour, he had to count people on and off the bus. That sort of thing. He decided to add disciplinarian to the role. It must have been a gesture of second-row solidarity with RH.

Anyway, up rose the Perk at the lunch table and started to upbraid the players for taking liberties. The younger ones, who had been told off before now by coach John Bevan for persistently coming in late, looked either blank or indignant themselves. I gently tugged on the Perk's sleeve.

'Shut up, Edwoot,' he said in his rich Blaenavon brogue. 'This is for me to sort out.' And on he raged. I tugged his sleeve again.

'What the . . .' shouted the preacher.

'Perk,' I said, 'it was us.' The old lags had had a bit of a session themselves the night before.

'As you were, men,' said the duty boy. 'On the bus in ten minutes.'

Manager R.H. Williams, a kind man. And coach, John Bevan, once of Aberavon as a player, now a coach. He had been an outside half at the same time as Phil Bennett, which had limited his number of caps. But he had been an innovative player and, something rare among number tens of those days, he had been extremely courageous in the tackle. In the Welsh win in Paris of 1975, a victory that would not be repeated until the age of Graham Henry twenty-four years later, he made a hair-raisingly brave tackle in the corner to save the day. He was good company too. In fact, there was a good feeling in the Welsh camp at that time.

John was innovative as a coach, seeking a high-tempo, fluid game. He was keen on fitness and many a beautiful morning on the costa near Valencia or on the high meseta around Valladolid was ruined by him flogging us in training. I think he was especially hard after the room-bill incident.

RH and Bev: neither would live for long after that tour. RH had a heart attack; John died of cancer.

The Lions had already declared themselves tired from their training in Hampshire. Nobody had expected anything else. There was a new steely edge to the management style. The word 'professional' would be used a thousand times on tour. And then some more. Presumably it featured large in the mission statement as a positive adjective, but it became the single word that would explain away any harshness. In the rugby of the new age 'professional' apparently granted licence to be a slave-driver.

'If you want a good time in Australia, then book a holiday there. After the tour,' was the grave riposte to any suggestion that the balance between pain and pleasure was not even lopsided but totally one-sided. A few players had already stopped smiling. They suspected that the Test team had already been chosen, that they were here merely to keep the midweek team-sheet full and provide cannon-fodder for the elite in yet more training.

We who were not even good enough to be first-choice dirt-trackers in 1983 had all been told to keep fit by the Lions, and John Bevan was doing his best to oblige. On the other hand, it was not easy for me. I had just recovered from a knee injury. Towards the end of the domestic season we had been building up to the climax of a first-ever appearance in the Cup Final against Swansea. In those days of only unofficial leagues, the Schweppes Challenge Cup was everything, and we had never won it.

We were playing out the fixtures of late April, with the Cup Final to be played in early May. Coventry had come to Ponty-pool Park and everything was going well enough until Chris Huish, our wing forward, grabbed hold of one of their players. Chris was known as 'Madman' and he, like the Perk, hailed from Blaenavon. We used to say you could tell which was Madman's house because it bowed in the middle, thanks to all the barbells and weights on his bedroom floor. Madman was rather strong.

I had a strong affection for Blaenavon. It lay five miles north of Pontypool in a slight bowl on the edge of the escarpment that rose steeply above the gentle, rolling pastures of the Vale of Usk. It was a harsher landscape up there on top of the Blorenge Mountain, and Blaenavon marked the start of industrial Wales. With its iron and steel works and coal pits, this was one of the cradles of industrial revolution. It was a town that was largely boarded up now, although its fortunes had recently improved with its elevation to World Heritage Site. It was one of those places where you could feel the goosebumps of history. It was here that a young alchemist called Gilchrist Thomas in a lost cottage somewhere on the mountainside first discovered the means of making steel from low-grade iron ore. He sold his basic Bessemer process to Andrew Carnegie in the United States in a deal that spelt in the long run the end for the high-grade steel-making villages and towns of Wales.

My grandfather had been a steelworker in Scunthorpe, but it

would be fanciful to say I was genetically drawn to Blaenavon. My father had been a research manager at the nylon factory in Pontypool and I had been brought up happily on the lush lowlands of Monmouthshire between the rivers Usk and Wye.

But I did like Blaenavon. It was a raw town. Some of the Pontypool players of the late seventies used to go training on Sunday mornings on the tramways that criss-crossed the mountainside above Forgeside, one of the town's three rugby clubs. We would change beforehand among the canaries in their cages in the shower-rooms of Big Pit, then still a working mine before it became a working museum.

Afterwards I would drive home on the road that drops vertiginously off the Blorenge down to Abergavenny, passing the Keepers Pond. This stretch of water was now a beauty spot, overlooking the south face of the Sugar Loaf, the most striking of the Black Mountains, but it too had an industrial history. From the Keepers Pond reservoir, three-inch pipes used to run back to the iron works of Blaenavon carrying water that would fill the tank of a balance tower. Thus would iron ore be raised towards the furnaces . . .

Much had been said and written about the changes in rugby between the amateur age and the professional era. Some of the Lions, like David Young at nearly thirty-four and Jason Leonard, going on thirty-three, were old enough to remember the amateur days of no payment at all. That was going back a bit, but the pair of props did. Props could do that. Others would have known the twilight days of amateurism in the 1990s, when illicit payments were commonplace. This was the age of semi-open hypocrisy, as opposed to the total hypocrisy that had gone with the very definition of amateurism. As soon as one single farmer said that he could not go on tour with his country, or even play for his club, because he could not afford to employ a locum dairyman, amateur rugby was guilty of discriminatory practices. Amateurism was designed to protect the gentleman player who had all the time in the world for travel and sport.

Most players on this Lions tour would have played during the

anarchic period that was triggered by the arrival of professionalism in 1995. Rugby union was caught on the hop when the
game turned pro. In the battles that followed and as people
fought for control of the finances – sorry, the soul of the game –
it was a wonder that nobody ended up seriously hurt. For rough
play, the committee room had been the place to be over the past
six years. The players and their coaches had saved the day. They
kept the crowds coming in by improving the game's playing
standards. Rugby could provide a true spectacle. It was not just a
game now for participants, but for spectators too. The value of
that spectator interest would be in remarkable evidence on the
tour of 2001.

Even as the Lions were in the air, disorder off the field was in
the process of becoming order. Peace was breaking out at the
Bastille of the game, Twickenham. Talk of structure and development had taken over from the sneer of 'Over my dead body'.
The players were still way ahead. They knew all about shape and
structure and development. The tourists of 2001 fully understood what being a dedicated athlete was all about. It was their
serious, well-paid job.

And yet, they were the same type of person that had always
been attracted to the game. Rugby was defined not by its pay
structures but by its nature. It offered opportunities to all shapes
and sizes and it demanded a high degree of co-operation between
them. It demanded all-round skills and specialist technique. It
was simple and yet it could be complicated, especially for its
thirty-first participant, the referee. It was loud and potentially
dangerous. Australia promised to be louder and more dangerous
than anywhere.

There I was playing against Coventry when Madman grabbed
hold of one of their players. The whistle went and I relaxed. But
Madman was in mid-swing and hurled the poor unfortunate
into the air. He landed on the outside of my right leg and
something yielded on the inside. The next thing I knew, I was
missing the Cup Final. There was a relevance to this. Lawrence
Dallaglio eighteen years later did a knee late in the English

domestic season, playing in the Zürich Championship semi-final between Wasps and Bath. He was doubtful for the Lions tour right up to the day of departure, and he left without being available for selection for the first three games. But if it was any consolation to him – and I didn't suppose it was – I could have told him, as I sat back, steeped in my nostalgic semi-conscious-ness and pork curry somewhere high over the Middle East, that just when you thought a bad knee would never mend, suddenly the ligaments tightened and you were up and running again.

Lawrence, had he been fit enough to run, would presumably have done so uncomplainingly. He had been a bit of a party animal in his time, and had been rolled over by the *News of the World* in a sting operation that placed him second only to Will Carling in the bracket of exposed high profile. But now he'd accepted the small print of being a star. If some of the players on tour were already feeling a chill wind of exclusion and exhaus-tion, then Lawrence and all the Test candidates – and perhaps they had been pre-picked – were going about their business with single-minded, head-down, just-get-on-with-it determination.

The pack around Martin Johnson was going to be basically English. Oak English with a few tough-nut Celts thrown in. Tom Smith of Scotland had done all this before, in South Africa, where some of the scrummaging sessions conducted by Jim Telfer in 1997 had reduced grown men to tears. And they were only the bystanders. Besides, nobody would know if the Scottish prop was unhappy or not on tour. Tom's style was Trappist. Or 'trappiste', as he might say – if he said anything, that is – because he'd been playing for Brive in France. No, Trappist. He'd just signed for Northampton.

Scott Quinnell of Wales had not played in a Test in South Africa and had come home injured from that mission. In fact, he had returned home accompanied by some wonderfully lurid stories about him having a fight with Martin Johnson. Which just went to show that players could always invent their own entertainment off the field. Or was it the press? Scott was back on a tour, keen to get it right this time. The playing side, he meant presumably.

Nobody had ever accused Keith Wood, fast becoming recognised as one of the greatest all-round practitioners of the hooking arts of all time, of not accepting a challenge. He had once made a stand, during that period of political anarchy in rugby, over the issue of his intellectual property rights. Basically, Woody had gone on strike and had not played for Ireland for a few games. There is no nobler beast in rugby than a principled hooker. He was as fast as a centre, and nearly as fast as the English hooker on tour, Phil Greening. Woody was from Limerick in Ireland, the son of Gordon, a Lion himself. He had gone to Harlequins when the job offers were coming in thick and fast at the start of the professional age, but had gone back to Munster on a sabbatical when the Harlequins well began to dry up. Back with his old province he had embarked on the great adventure of 2000 that saw Munster go all the way to the European Cup Final. They lost to Northampton, but the next year he was back with Harlequins and winning the European Shield. He did love a challenge. Ireland's captain had been in South Africa in 1997, too.

As had second row Jeremy Davidson, who had stepped up at a time of concern on that tour over the line-out and scrummage, to claim his part in the success story there. The front five of the Lions pack of 1997 had ended up with a decidedly non-English look to it. Only Martin Johnson had found a place.

But the heart of this tour's pack was expected to be English. Phil Greening, Phil Vickery, Danny Grewcock, plus the captain himself would be strong contenders. Jason Leonard provided cover for both sides of the front row. And in the back row, England could promote the talents of Dallaglio, Richard Hill and Neil Back. None of these forwards was going to complain about unremitting hard work when they shared the belief of their captain that any success enjoyed by England was precisely the result of unremitting hard work. Neil Back probably thought the training wasn't hard enough.

I missed the Cup Final of 1983. Pontypool won what was generally considered to be the most boring game of all time.

As if we cared. But just a few days later the knee was no longer wobbly and I was off on tour with Wales B to Spain. Where my back went. I managed to play on but came home in a spasm of inflexibility, and the only training I could do for the rest of the summer was to churn up and down the swimming pool of Cheltenham College where I was employed as a teacher. Ah, those amateur days. Life was all about exams and umpiring Under-14 cricket. And then, just as term was drawing to a close, I became the latest and last player to be called up to go on the Lions tour to New Zealand. Before I could say, 'Well, actually, I've got a bit of a dodgy . . .' I was on the plane bound for Auckland.

In truth, by the time I landed in New Zealand there were only eight days to go. I reckoned I could bluff my way through them. They were eight long days. Playing for the Lions was fantastic. All those things you heard about pride and honour and being special were true. But it did help if the Lions were winning. The 1983 brand was not. They were 0–3 down in the four-Test series and they all wanted to come home. This wasn't tour of mutiny, just multiple muggings.

This might have helped my cause a bit. If they wanted to be gone from there, perhaps there might be a place up for grabs. In the Test team even. Bad back or no bad back. 'I'm sorry you've had a wasted journey,' said coach Jim Telfer at Auckland Airport. 'But John Beattie and Iain Paxton are both fit.' The two players I had come out to replace were no longer in need of being replaced. 'Ach, now you're here you may as well stay.' Yes, playing for the Lions was special.

We went straight from the airport to Pukekohe. By now it was Saturday lunchtime and there was a game to play against Counties. Graham Price, also of Pontypool and now on his third Lions tour, filled me in on just how tough the going was. He had been to New Zealand in 1977, and so powerful had the Lions pack been at that time that they had reduced the All Blacks to putting just three forwards into the scrummage. Now it was the Lions' turn to be on the receiving end. 'They're booting us from one end of the country to the other,' was the great tight-head prop's verdict.

A couple of hours after landing I was sitting on the replacements' bench. Ach, you may as well stay had become ach, we might as well give you something to do while you're here. I was not required to perform, which was a bit of a relief. I know I should have been itching to get out there and all that, but I seemed to have adopted the shape of an economy-class plane seat. I was pleased not to have to try to jump in a line-out. And I was not exactly thrilled when the subs were ordered to go jogging after the end of the game.

As we toured the perimeter of the field spectators began to pick us off. Over the railings they came and started to tackle us from behind. Down went Colin Deans of Scotland. Down went Ginger McLoughlin of Ireland.

On the third occasion we retaliated. I must say I formed quite a mean partnership with Ginger. He wrestled them to the floor and I ran in and put the boot in. And I might add that as therapy for a stiff back it was an effective exercise. The headlines next day across New Zealand and back home in the *South Wales Argus* ran something like 'Lions in Shameful Brawl'.

And that was about it really on my first Lions tour. I played in the following game against Waikato, which we won. And then I provided token opposition for the Test team in their build-up to the final Test at Eden Park, Auckland. Which the Lions lost. And how. 6–38, a record defeat for the Lions. Even though I had been away for only eight days, it was good to go home.

Behind the scrum there was going to be a rare old contest at scrum half. Now, the characters here were not quite as uncomplaining as the forwards. Meek compliance would not apply to any of the following: Rob Howley, Matt Dawson and Austin Healey. This is just a flavour of their spikiness. Rob had fallen out with Graham Henry himself and had had the captaincy of Wales taken off him. Then, when David Young was injured, Rob turned down the offer of doing the job again. He found he had lost not only the captaincy, but also his very place. It went to Rupert Moon of Llanelli who gave it his all, as always, to the point of being inspirational. But given the form Rob was displaying in 2001, this blip in 2000 seemed an aberration of absurd proportions. It even suggested that the coach could be quite vindictive if a player did not do exactly as he was told. Rob, in compliance with the Lions' code of conduct, was giving nothing away as he travelled to Australia, but his experiences suggested that Henry did have an appetite for control.

Matt Dawson had been captain of England and had been dropped by England. For years he had had a running contest with Kyran Bracken for the number nine shirt. He had been number two to Rob Howley in South Africa, only to become heroic number one when Rob dislocated a shoulder. He was an active television pundit and had strong opinions.

Austin Healey was the third scrum half. Graham Henry had insisted back at the Heathrow announcement that he was only going as a scrum half. How this sat with Austin remained to be seen. Some days he liked scrum half. On others he liked only outside half. Or wing. He had started in the European Cup Final for Leicester at scrum half and in the closing moments had ended up at outside half, from where he made the break that led to the try that won the game that made the Tigers the champions of Europe.

As the team and the fans went crazy at the end of the game, Austin grabbed the microphone. He thanked the Tigers' supporters for travelling all the way to the Parc des Princes. This was one in the eye for the organisers who had brought them to the neutral venue of Paris to play against Stade Français. Of Paris.

On his return to Leicester Austin said he was going to leave the club unless they played him at outside half. Then he changed his mind. He was excellent value. I was not really obliged to say that, but it helped. The Leicester and England player was going to be a contributor to the *Guardian* and the *Observer*, and I was going to ghost-write his columns for him.

Even as we were in the air flying to Australia it was not hard to predict that at some stage words would be exchanged between management and at least a couple of the huddle of scrum halves.

My second Lions trip came in 1993. By now I had moved into journalism, having had five years with BBC Wales in Cardiff. That first stint in broadcasting had ended in tears and I was now writing for the *Observer*. We were back in New Zealand, although this time I was there for the whole ten-week trip.

New Zealand was a nightmare for a player. For a non-player it was brilliant. The weather that southern winter was mild, the landscapes were varied and dramatic, the golf courses were universally welcoming, the hotels were fine, the food was good and the rugby was nearly riveting. But not quite.

The midweek team of that year made the Lions of 1983 seem like world-beaters. They became the laughing stock of NZ. They simply stopped trying, which did not go down well in the land where competitive spirit is as naturally big as a Maori thigh. Fortunately, the first team fared better. This was a tour of them in midweek and us on the weekend. The Saturday team were robbed in the first Test in Christchurch, won the second in Wellington and only came unstuck in the decider in Auckland. On the big day the All Blacks, who faced being lynched if they lost, found the thrust they had been lacking. Despite conceding an early try after a clattering break by Scott Gibbs, they ran out winners 30–13. To win a Lions series you had to able to match the southern hemisphere teams' single-minded will to win. You had to share their fear of failure.

At outside half it was impossible to imagine Jonny Wilkinson leading a revolution. The scrum halves might be recalcitrant, but not Jonny. He represented unflappable, sincere quality. And that would do nicely. Ronan O'Gara and Neil Jenkins provided the cover at ten, but if Jonny was fit Jonny would play. He played like some hoary oracle who'd been playing for England for a hundred years or more. He'd just celebrated his twenty-second birthday.

There were some fitness doubts wider out. Mike Catt had not played for some time. There was much excitement nonetheless about the potential of his partnership with Brian O'Driscoll. Mike had a right boot to complement Jonny's left and a touch of madness to balance Jonny's eminently sound level-headedness. Together they had crafted the extravagant moves in the England back division. Brian O'Driscoll, lightning off the mark and artfully well-balanced, might be inspired by the chemistry. Or not. Who could tell? The backs had to be the unknown factor. And who could discount Will Greenwood, who knew his fellow England players' habits better than anyone? If England were to provide the bulk of the forwards, why not the core of the three-quarters?

Jim Telfer and Ian McGeechan, the coaches of 1983 and 1993, learned their lessons. They combined to form the most driven coaching partnership the rugby players of Britain and Ireland had ever seen when they took the Lions of 1997 to South Africa. It was a fantastic tour. The very concept of the Lions had been called into question when the game went professional in 1995. This tour reaffirmed the Lions' special place in the world game. It put European rugby back on the map. Its defining image was of Scott Gibbs overrunning the massive Springbok prop Os Du Randt. In his time Scott had done a fair bit of clattering. The Test series was sensational.

And I missed it. Having done the Lions tour of '93 and the World Cup of 1995 in South Africa, I had decided that I wanted to branch out into areas other than rugby. It was my Hemingway moment. Very well, the *Observer* said. And two months later I was sacked in a round of cutbacks. These were troubled times for the paper; and they weren't exactly brilliant for me either.

Mercifully, the bloke responsible for my dismissal, Andrew Jaspan, did not survive long as editor. After he went I was given my old job back. Even more mercifully, under Roger Alton, the *Observer* recovered and a couple of years later here I was, off again on my third Lions tour.

If the combinations in midfield were the unknown quantity on the tour of 2001, what was going to happen out wide and at full

back? Dan Luger, with no fear of sharing some of the players'
chronic fatigue at the end of a long domestic season, had to
regain match-fitness. Jason Robinson was hardly going to be
worn out either. The player used by England in short bursts off
the replacements' bench had very little experience of a full rugby
union game of eighty minutes. They were both left wingers, as
were Dafydd James and Ben Cohen. There seemed to be a lot of
left wingers on the trip and not a lot of right. Iain Balshaw could
always play there. He had more experience of playing on the
wing than he had at fullback. But he was the sensation of the
moment at number fifteen, running from deep and giving
England the cutting edge for which they had been yearning
for a long time. Matt Perry was the other fullback on tour, and
there was no question that he had a lot more experience than
Iain. It was just that Iain could run frighteningly fast. Everybody
was looking forward to seeing him play on the dry tracks of
Australia.

We landed in Bangkok and stepped out into a wall of heat. It was
only a brief stop before the next plane took us on to Perth. I
found myself talking to Lee Smith, a New Zealander who
worked for the International Rugby Board as director of development. He was on his way to Sri Lanka where he was to
conduct a workshop on the seven-a-side game. We talked about
declining player numbers in British Columbia and the general
collapse of the game in Romania. And then we found ourselves
discussing the merits of man-to-man marking George Gregan,
the Wallaby scrum half. It was funny, the things you could talk
about in transit lounges.

   Such a conversation in Bangkok helped concentrate the mind
on the opposition. The Wallabies. How to beat the best? What
lessons could be taken from the last Lions tour, to South Africa?
The tour of 1997 had been successful, but in all truth, the
Springboks of that year were not at their peak. They were
caught in an interregnum between the coaching eras of Kitch
Christie, under whom they had won the World Cup in 1995, and
Nick Mallett, who between 1997 and 1998 would steer them to

seventeen Test victories. That run gave them a share of the world record for consecutive Test wins. The in-between age of Carel Du Plessis was short-lived. The Lions helped end it by going 2–0 up in the series, before losing the third Test. The Springboks were as physically aggressive and obdurate as ever, but lacked cohesion and an overall strategy. This was going to be different. The Wallabies were master thinkers on the game. Sound theory had led to many practical rewards. They were holders of every title going. But cool-headed investigative analysis was allied to their hot-humoured inheritance. The treatment handed out by the Lions on their last tour of Australia was scorched on the Wallaby mind. The current team were torch-bearers for the wounded Aussies of 1989 and were expected to exact revenge for what had happened a dozen years previously. It was a one-off opportunity. Few of them, if any, would be around to play against the next Lions, due to tour Australia in 2013.

David Campese, who had scored in usually outrageous style a world-record number of tries, sixty-four, in his 101 Tests, was wheeled out of retirement to relive one of his not so glorious moments. Campo, whom I had chased very much in vain in the Wales–Australia game of 1984, had gifted Ieuan Evans the try that swung the series of 1989 the Lions way. It was not a pretty moment for the great wing. He had tried to run from behind his own line, had advanced a couple of metres and had tried to find his fullback Greg Martin with a pass. It missed. Ieuan of Llanelli and Wales fell on the ball and Campo had never quite lived it down.

Now he found himself in a television commercial, sitting on one end of a sofa. On the other sat the Bundaberg Rum mascot, a giant polar bear. They were watching a re-run of the 1989 try. 'Never mind, mate,' said the bear. 'Pass me a cold one, will you?' Campo reached down for a beer and threw it at the bear. It missed, of course, and went through the window. Campo and polar bear shrugged. Not every evocation of the series of 1989 was blood-curdling.

The Wallabies of the new age had world-class halfbacks in George Gregan and Stephen Larkham. George was both abrasive and silky smooth. He had made one of the best tackles ever seen in his first year of Test rugby. It was 1994. Campo was still playing but his opposite number, Jeff Wilson of New Zealand, had escaped and was in the act of diving for the line to score the try that would have retained possession of the Bledisloe Cup for the All Blacks. Out of nowhere George Gregan hit him with a covering tackle. The ball was dislodged and the Wallabies instead won and regained the Cup. Since then, Australia's scrum half had grown only better on all fronts, including his lightning service and even his defence. George was pint-sized but he epitomised the combative spirit of the Wallaby camp.

Stephen Larkham had done something equally special in his career. The 1999 World Cup semi-final against the Springboks at Twickenham had gone into extra time, the scores having been level after eighty minutes. Stephen was not a kicker. Obviously he could put boot to ball, but he was much more renowned as a sound reader of the game and as a slinky distributor of a pass. Suddenly from near the halfway line he sent over the most sensational drop goal. It was very difficult to put Stephen Larkham or any of the Wallabies into a pigeonhole.

They had options at fullback, with either Matt Burke or Chris Latham, both large and rapid. In the centre they had someone even more solid in Daniel Herbert. Joe Roff was just as large and even faster on the left wing.

Up front they had a class second-row pairing in David Giffin and the incomparable John Eales, who had played in the toughest, roughest madhouse of a position for over a decade and yet remained the sweetest, kindest man on the planet. Jeremy Paul at hooker had been playing superbly for the ACT Brumbies, and if he did not make the team they had cover in the shape of Michael Foley, who might not make the bracket of sweet and kind. The props might be a problem, if only because the Wallabies were worried about a lack of depth. An old guard had retired. Would Glen Panoho and Nick Stiles have the wiliness to combat the Lions?

Nor was there much experience on the open side in the back row. But George Smith was a twenty-year-old sensation who was expected to be one of the stars of the series. Accompanying him would be two from three: Toutai Kefu at number eight, strong and forceful, and either Owen Finegan, equally muscular, or Matt Cockbain, rangier and more adept at line-out work.

There would be no Ben Tune on the left wing, which was good news for the Lions. The outstanding wing was even more plagued by injury than Dan Luger. The player expected to replace him, Andrew Walker, was a convert from league. If ever he came up against Jason Robinson, their contest was expected to give off sparks.

There might just be a hole for the Lions to exploit somewhere between Stephen Larkham and Daniel Herbert. Stirling Mortlock was injured. Who would the Wallabies go for: Elton Flatley or Nathan Grey? The Lions would view that selection with interest.

Graham Henry had said he had spotted a few weaknesses. Did he mean it? In 1971 the Lions went to New Zealand, where Carwyn James immediately announced he knew precisely where the All Blacks could be beaten. Apparently at that stage he did not have a clue, but it sent the home team into such a spin that a vital psychological march had been stolen. Graham Henry knew about Lions tours from the receiving end. New Zealanders were meticulous students of the game. Had he really unearthed a point of weakness, or was he sprinkling some moonshine?

5

Perth

We began to descend over the blackness of Western Australia, towards Perth. Blaenavon was a long way away. Quite what I had thought the worn-out Welsh town might have in common with Perth began to escape me as this final leg of the outward journey drew to a close. Mining perhaps? The exhausted supplies of coal and iron ore and limestone from that speck of a town in a land the size of a pinhead against gold and uranium from the vast expanses of Australia's largest state? It was stretching an unlikely connection. Isolation perhaps? Blaenavon sat perched on the edge of its escarpment, geographically only a few miles from the plain below, but somehow also light years distant. Perth lay on its own, separated from the rest of the world by thousands of miles of ocean, polar continent, desert or scrub. Melbourne was three and a half hours away by plane, while a journey to Sydney on the Indian–Pacific railway took three days.

It appeared Perth might outdo Blaenavon on most fronts, including wealth. The city stretched gracefully along the banks of the Swan River. Fremantle, the old working port that was spruced up not so long ago for the America's Cup, lay at the south entrance to the estuary, while the skyline of the Perth business district rose affluently upstream on the north bank. The millionaire residences along the Swan suggested that this was indeed a long way from the terraced rows of old South Wales.

We arrived at midnight and headed for the Duxton Hotel.

This building used to be a tax office, which was not altogether encouraging. But it turned out to have been totally refurbished. The management moreover were prepared to keep the bar open in order to service our jet lag.

Of all things, we talked about the weather. How to prevent George Gregan and Stephen Larkham from running the show against the Lions gave way to small talk about how chilly it was.

But it was. The locals were at a loss to explain it. The Fremantle Doctor was a welcome summer breeze that brought a cooling draught up from Antarctica, but a stationary and decidedly frosty front had settled over wintry Perth. So much for the Mediterranean climate.

Having gone to bed at 2 a.m. and been wide awake at four, I was struggling by the time it came to the first official deed of the tour; the ten o'clock press conference at the Lions' hotel in Fremantle and the announcement of the team for the first match, against Western Australia on Friday night. It was hardly the most dramatic fanfare to adventure. Rugby press conferences are the scrubbed and wholesome face of a sport that can still generate its share of dirtiness, not to say filth. As we had seen in Heathrow, the sponsors' logos came before any verbal worth. From Twickenham to Auckland the press conferences are stage-managed, spun and sanitised, microcosms of press briefings in real life. Nothing even remotely approaching a smidgen of indiscretion escapes. They are normally inordinately dull.

Graham Henry's in Australia promised to be no more exciting than those he gave elsewhere. The coach gave nothing away apart from the team list and a few preambles that you would expect about the challenge ahead. The wingers were to be Ben Cohen and Dan Luger. How, Henry was asked, had it been decided that one of them should move to the right?

'Oh, they decided amongst themselves,' said the coach dead casually.

Paul Morgan, editor of the magazine *Rugby World*, happened to see Ben Cohen five minutes later. 'So, you had a chat with Dan about who would play where, did you?' asked the editor.

'What are you talking about?' said the right wing. 'We do as we're told.'

I had a couple of hours to kill in Fremantle. At 10.30 I had telephoned Austin Healey to make an appointment. He had groaned and said he was asleep. Worn out. In bed. Come back at one o'clock, he said. Goodbye.

Austin was an interesting bloke. He would be useless at press conferences, since he liked to tell you what he thought. I had been collared by him a couple of times. Once in Bloemfontein he had scoffed at my skinny legs, and, late one night in the Atlantic Bar in Soho back in London, he had said that his mother would shoot me if she ever got her hands on me. Or rather, on a gun. She kept all his press cuttings, as mums tend to do – mine did too, to send to Aunt Alma in Enderby – and reckoned I had written some disparaging things about her boy.

Now, I probably had. Austin had been an eccentric player over the years, and not everything he attempted came off. But – and I swear this is true – I had always felt, and I thought I had always written, that he should be in the England team. He could not just play almost anywhere but he could also play there with daring and vision. He was a specialist utility player, or an all-round specialist, whether at scrum half, outside half or wing.

Having noted that the Lions' hotel, the Esplanade, was promoting a week-long Croatian food festival in late June in its Atrium Restaurant, I wandered around Fremantle with Robert Kitson of the *Guardian*. We braved an outdoor coffee in the cold sunshine and said how nice it was to be on tour. I told him I was doing Austin Healey. 'Glad it's you,' he said. 'We've had our run-ins. He told me once his mum wanted to shoot me . . .'

I went back to the team hotel and at one o'clock on the dot Austin appeared. He did look tired. In fact, he spelt out how tired he was in detail, how they were being flogged twice a day in training. Especially by Phil Larder the defence coach. The players all knew they had to cram in the work, but that didn't stop them being absolutely knackered. He'd be glad when they could actually start playing matches. He was on the bench for Friday, which gave him two more days to fleece everyone else at three-card brag. And win more at the casino. Three hundred dollars he'd won the night before, on Caribbean stud poker and blackjack. And he'd found the cinema that sold the best popcorn in Fremantle. He didn't go to the cinema for the films, just the popcorn. Now, if I'd excuse him, he had to go back to bed.

Writing columns for players was not always the most rewarding of duties. But this was going to be different. I was going to make Mrs Healey put away her firearm.

It wasn't just the players Phil Larder was working hard. At the hotel I also bumped into Alun Carter, the video analyst with the team. Alun had once been a team-mate at Pontypool, where he was known as 'Spring' for his party-piece of being able to bounce into the air from a cross-legged position without apparently moving a muscle. He later moved down to Newport to have more opportunities of first-team rugby. From there he won a couple of caps in the Welsh back row in 1991. He had been a mobile wing forward who, while with us, used to engage in races, which became classics of their kind, with Mark Brown, our regular open-side. Mark was six feet four inches tall, as thin as a rake and could have been an international 400-metre runner. We used to call his stride pattern 'Whispering Death'. We would begin training with four laps of Pontypool Park, the last of which was a run for home. A race. As everyone gasped around the scoreboard bend into the back straight, Mark would come gliding silently through. Only Spring could live with him, and even he had to give way on the home sprint. The rest of us flailed in a long way back.

Alun in those days was a policeman. It was hard to believe now. We once went on tour to Toronto where the young constable kept setting off the fire alarm. Well, he did it twice. The fire service and the hotel management were not best impressed and Spring was issued with a final warning. Once more, and you're on your way home. Try explaining that to the Chief Constable.

Spring sought solace in shopping and came home one afternoon with a gift for his nephew, a helicopter that went round
and round on the end of a plastic line. He decided on a test-flight,
but could not affix the end of the line into the hard artex ceiling
of his room. So, he stuck the pin in the only available material
with a bit of give in it, which happened to be the surround of the
smoke-detector.

The fire service found him cowering beneath his sheets. 'I
don't want to go home,' he was wailing. We took pity on him, if
only because we seemed to be a bit light on players, half the team
having flown down to New York for a Phil Collins concert. The
balance between pain and pleasure on that tour might have
swung the other way.

Alun Carter was busy now in Perth, filming the training
sessions and editing them for Phil Larder and the forwards
coach, Andy Robinson. More and more footage was required.
Details of angles of running here and body positions there. Alun,
like Austin, was tired.

Come to think of it, I wasn't exactly feeling brilliant myself. Jet
lag was creeping up. I caught the Transperth commuter train
back from Fremantle to the centre of town. It offered a brief
scene of interest with a host of fishermen crowding the concrete
bases beneath the Stirling Freeway Bridge, but then we began to
run through the suburbs of West Perth with a rhythm guaranteed to make even the brightest-eyed office-worker drowsy.

Somewhere on the Fremantle side of the Swan the Lions
would be training again. At least they now had a focus. The
team to play on Friday night would no longer be going through
the routines with a sense of being on automatic pilot, but in the
knowledge that what they were rehearsing might directly affect
the way they played on the night. One good performance and
they would have, as Graham Henry put it, 'put up a hand'. The
Test team might have been pre-selected in theory but there could
be no denying repeated shows of top form on tour. And where
better to start to make an impression than in the opening game?

Likewise, it could all go wrong. One indifferent game right at
the very outset and that could be the entire trip ruined. For many

players this might be their one and only chance. There was bound to be some apprehension, however humble the opposition.

The selectors were not taking the challenge of Western Australia so seriously that they were putting out all their big guns. WA were pure warm-up material. Perth was not a rugby hotbed. The city's Australian Rules clubs were reporting record losses as well. Rugby league didn't really feature this far west. What did they do out here in the winter? Somebody said that the biggest sport in June was the trotting at Gloucester Park, right next door to the WACA.

Martin Johnson was not playing. The captain had had a bit of a congested end of the season, what with Leicester winning the two Zürich competitions and the European Cup Final. He had told me in Stockport that he was really quite fresh because England's international programme had been disrupted by the foot and mouth epidemic. And before that unexpected mid-season break he'd enjoyed a five-week holiday because of suspension. In a club match against Saracens he had crushed a few ribs belonging to Duncan McRae.

Funnily enough, McRae was here in Australia. Or, he was back in Australia, for this was home. He was a utility rugby player, having played league for three years with the Canterbury Bulldogs in Sydney and having filled just about every position in the union back line. He was going to sign a contract with the New South Wales Waratahs. But before that, and this was even funnier, he was here in Perth, sitting on the Western Australia bench, ready to face the Lions, if not the player who'd handed him – or kneed him – a mid-season break of his own.

In the place of the tour captain was Danny Grewcock, who moved up from number five to four. In 1995 Danny had had a season in Perth, playing with the Cottesloe club. Scotland's Scott Murray, who wasn't named in the team for Friday, had also played here, for Western Suburbs. Two Lions knew Perth better than Duncan McRae.

In the middle of the line-out would be Malcolm O'Kelly, the tall Irishman, who played for St Mary's in Dublin. The front row had 'Test' inked all over it: Phil Vickery of Gloucester, Keith Wood of Harlequins, who was also captain for the night, and Darren Morris, the burly Swansea loose-head whom we expected at this stage to have the edge over Tom Smith.

It was too early to read too much into any of the selections, and Graham Henry had clearly said that there was no point in even trying. Not that that stopped us in the press gang. The back row, with the proviso that Lawrence Dallaglio would not be in contention for at least three games, also had a serious look to it: Richard Hill, Neil Back and Scott Quinnell.

Rob Howley had the first crack at scrum half. And from then on, it all went a little peculiar. Ronan O'Gara was playing, presumably because all the Irish in the party, having seen their rugby dry up because of foot and mouth, needed as much rugby as possible, as soon as possible. That had to be why Brian O'Driscoll was selected at fullback. 'How many times have you played there, Brian?' the centre had been asked. 'Never,' was the easy answer. No, Western Australia were not anticipated to be the most awesome rugby team on the planet.

With O'Driscoll on duty behind them, the centres were to be Mark Taylor and Will Greenwood. Mark was as sensible as they come, a Welsh version of Jonny Wilkinson. As a former Pontypool player, not a bad word could ever be said about him. Will had bleached his hair white, could play inside or outside and had made a staggering return to top-flight rugby after suffering a horrendous blow to his head on the South African tour of 1997. He had tried playing at Leicester after the injury but it was only on his return to Harlequins that he rediscovered his willowy skills. Taking the tackle and slipping the ball out of it was his speciality.

The two lefties, Dan Luger and Ben Cohen, were on the wings. The ones who had decided things for themselves by obeying orders. Such was the first team to play on tour. And they were all going through their moves with a new tingle of anticipation.

Meanwhile I was asleep on the Transperth. I had a habit of falling asleep on trains. Returning from London I had swept and slept through Bristol Parkway as far as Taunton and Bridgend.

Even awake, I could land in trouble. I once watched Lydney come and go, forgetting I was supposed to alight there. My worst moment came when I was travelling to Bath, who were playing at home against London Scottish. The train journey from Newport lasted barely three-quarters of an hour, but off I dropped. I woke up as we were pulling out of Bath Spa. 'No reason to panic,' I thought. 'Chippenham will do. A quick about-turn; no problem. Swindon even. Might make it a bit tight, but it can be done.' The next stop turned out to be Reading.

I missed kick-off neatly by eighty minutes. I arrived back at the Recreation Ground, just a stone's throw from Bath Spa Station, as the crowd was spilling out. Brian Oliver was brand new in the job of sports editor at the *Observer*. He could have sacked me without ever having met me. Like Alun Carter, I knew the value of forgiveness.

I jumped out at Perth as the train doors were closing. Otherwise I was heading for Guildford, the town that marks the start of the Swan Valley wine region. Not that an extended journey to such a place was without its attractions . . . but no, I had decided that if I was going to tackle jet lag head-on it was best done in company. So, back to the Duxton it was. And deep into the night the press corps drank, all in the interests of a good night's sleep.

I woke at midday on Thursday, which meant I had been out for eight hours. This was such a rarity that I celebrated by immediately putting on shorts, trainers and T-shirt and heading off for a run on the cycle-path that followed the Swan towards the sea.

I was finding, as I grew older, that long bouts of sleep evaded me. I often awoke in the middle of the night and generally my thoughts in the early hours were rather bleak. Any decent, positive, creative bursts tended to come to me when I was mowing the lawn at home. Very Voltairian, I know, and it meant that I leant towards what I imagined was a Scandinavian glumness about the winter. Travelling away from my beloved few fractions of an acre of grass and garden made me apprehensive about the balance of my spirits. Especially since, at the very moment when the lawn began to spurt, I more often than not found myself packing my bags and heading towards the winter of the southern hemisphere.

Without claiming to be Forrest Gump, I enjoy running. I like the mental emptiness it brings. The only thoughts that go through my head as I lollop along are to do with purely bodily responses, even if the loudest of these is pain. I like ticking off a check-list of targets and I love most of all the aerobic high that comes after exercise. Running after an eight-hour sleep seemed to me to be a perfect opportunity to build up some credit in the fight against my Scandinavian syndrome. So, off I set. Half an hour later I reached some pitches outside a natty clubhouse sporting the name Nedlands Rugby Club. Like an ageing walrus marking his territory, I deposited some mucus beneath a tree, turned around and headed back towards the Perth skyline.

The return journey was not easy. A rhythm was hard to find. Perth remained agonisingly distant. At one stage, in the opposite direction, came Steve Bale, rugby correspondent at the *Express* and a regular runner on tour. As far back as 1993 we would pass each other on the pathways through the mango swamps of the Bay of Islands in New Zealand. We once dodged rats while circumnavigating a lake in Bucharest. He waved his arms and shouted apologies for something he had said the night before. My head was empty of everything bar dear old pain. I had no recall of any incident. I'm sure it was not serious. Spats were the bread and butter of journalists a long way from home. And what you could remember you could not condemn. People in the business of dispensing justice should go out running. High Court judges should pound the roads before passing sentence. I grunted at Steve in the fashion of a pardon on the hoof. More mucus tumbled out and I plodded on.

That evening I went out with Alastair Hignell, the rugby commentator for BBC radio. Alastair and I were at Cambridge University together. When I arrived at Fitzwilliam College in 1976 he was in his third year. I was reading Modern Languages and he History. I had half a dozen games for Pontypool under my belt; Alastair had already played for England.

He had arrived in Cambridge as a scrum half but had converted so easily to fullback that he had gone on England's 1975 tour to Australia. This was a trip that had passed into the annals not so much for the courageous tackling of the young convert but for the wildness of the brawls that broke out at regular intervals in front of him among the gnarled forwards. In the second Test prop Mike Burton was sent off, the first Englishman to be dismissed in international rugby. If 1989 had been violent, it was nothing compared with the mayhem of 1975. The Australians did not seem to hark back to '75 so much, perhaps because they won that particular fight. 1989 was more the Gallipoli spirit. Hail the campaigns lost.

Alastair was the most gifted sportsman of his generation. He had won Blues as a freshman in both rugby and cricket. He was already playing county cricket for Gloucestershire. It all came to him with ridiculous ease. He was an unlikely-looking sporting hero: bearded, squat, scuttling and with plenty of bottom right hand in his batting. But he was truly blessed with a hand-eye coordination and sense of timing that few possessed. He did not run now. Alastair had multiple sclerosis.

When it became known that he had been diagnosed with MS a series of dinners was organised, to raise funds for Interferon, a drug not available on the National Health Service. Medical opinion was apparently divided as to whether it did, as was claimed and hoped, effectively slow down the disease. While the politicians and doctors argued, it just seemed to those who knew Alastair that any attempt to tame the beast was worth making. The first big fundraiser was held at the Café Royal in London. It was the full black-tie number. All the tables had been snapped up by the rugby, cricket and broadcasting fraternities. The England rugby team were to attend. And so was a gang of Alastair's old mates from Cambridge days, including me.

It just so happened I had to go to London earlier in the day, for a spot of think-tanking at the *Observer*. These were irregular meetings but were very, very important. Sports correspondents and contributors would come in from yards away and would normally stay sober for about half an hour before adjourning to the Coach and Horses.

During the course of that particular afternoon we did scratch down on the back of some beermats a few notes as to who might be doing what in the forthcoming weeks, but it was also true to say that we gave it a bit of a lash.

An hour in a pub in Glasshouse only made things worse. I was steered to the Café Royal. On the way across the ballroom floor I passed the BBC table. 'Ah, Eddie, meet our new head of sport,' they all cried. 'Eddie this is Peter Salmon. Peter, Eddie, one of our rugby commentators.' I tried to speak and they very considerately ushered me away.

The night was long and hard. Everybody at the Cambridge table was enormously successful in business or the law. Some had even accumulated enough to retire at an absurdly young age. Faced with this, I could only keep drinking.

The auction to raise funds went on and on. It was the essential part of the evening, but the longer it lasted the more I felt – in a numbed sort of way, you understand – that this was all rather mercenary. And that somehow the sums were taking over from the human side of the situation. This was Alastair, our own Higgy, we were talking about. He wasn't up for sale.

'Finally, ladies and gentlemen,' announced Ian Robertson, the BBC rugby correspondent who had also been our coach at Cambridge, 'if I could just call on one last speaker to round off the evening and tell you what a fantastic chap Alastair is . . . please step forward Eddie Butler.'

Oh my. I decided to re-humanise Alastair by telling everyone how we'd abandoned him one year on the Paris–Epernay express, naked as the day he was born. It had seemed so amusing at the time. How he couldn't kick goals to save his life, especially in the Varsity match of 1977 when we were red-hot favourites to win. He'd had so many pain-killing injections in his ankle that he couldn't feel a thing. We lost.

It's dangerous allowing people to do things in public when they're anaesthetised. Sorry, Alastair.

It could have been more embarrassing. Luckily, Peter Salmon, the new head of BBC Sport, did not stay for the speeches. And fortunately, the England team, bless them, were on strike that night. They turned up – a wonderful gesture in itself – but shut themselves away in a room after dinner for emergency talks with their management.

And, although the memory was one of those bleak thoughts that woke me in the early hours, it couldn't have been too bad. Alastair asked me to speak at his next two functions. 'Personally, I don't care what they all said about you,' he said. 'At the time, I thought you were quite amusing.'

We went out that night in Perth with Nigel Breakey, who had played with us in Cambridge. In that 1977 game we lost, actually. Nigel was now an anaesthetist in Perth. We went first to Swanbourne Rugby Club and met a few rugby-loving doctors who were in Perth for a conference on Critical Care. I looked rather anxiously at Alastair but he was leaning quite happily on his walking stick. Then we went, in a smaller group of medicos, to a Zimbabwean steakhouse. Alastair and Nigel sat at one end and got stuck into the old days. I found myself sitting with Peter and Judith, a couple who had emigrated to Perth from Cape Town in 1978. Peter was out of medicine now, and dabbling in all sorts of interesting property and wine ventures. He wanted the international press to launch a crusade against the Australian Rugby Union, demanding to know on what grounds Western Australia had been allocated no tickets for the Tests. Why, a friend of theirs had had to queue for six hours in Melbourne to ensure that they would be able to attend the second Test.

The next day was Friday. It was time for the Lions' first game at last. Match days were quiet for the press. Rarely was there anything to file until the game had been played. Kick-off was not until the evening, giving us the whole day to kill.

Twenty-five of that family of photographers, commentators, reporters and writers went down in the morning to the Royal Perth Yacht Club. This had been the centre of operations at the time of the Alan Bond adventure in the America's Cup. It was a club catering for serious sailing folk and they were prepared to give the media a go on some of their finest racing boats.

We were divided up into teams, based loosely on nationality. Crewing our particular thirty-six-footer were Paul Morgan of *Rugby World*, Andy Howell of the *Western Mail*, Graham Thomas of BBC Wales, Graham Clutton of the Westgate Sports Agency in Cardiff and myself. Our coach was a more local Graham, an experienced hand on the ocean wave, who also ran a fitness club in the suburbs. He gave us a brief but intensive lesson on the need for teamwork. I thought he was going to plagiarise the Lions' mission statement at one point but he quickly changed tack to safety considerations, wind, sails and other matters salty. As somebody who had sat in Rushcutters Bay for the BBC during the Sydney Olympics and presented the daily dramas of Ben Ainsley, Shirley Robertson, the 49-ers and the Soling class among others from the successful British sailing team, I tried to appear to know what he was talking about. But I didn't. Not a clue. I am a landlubber with the seafaring instincts of a Swiss mountain-guide, who would have melted in terror in Rushcutters Bay had it not been for the comforting presence alongside me of Hugh Stiles, skipper of the Tornado-class catamaran.

Not that any depth of knowledge was necessary on the morning of the Lions' first game. Perth Water stretched before us, crystal-clear and undisturbed by even a feather-duster ripple. A starting line was prepared and one of the coaches tried to work out how far we might progress in roughly one hour of racing. The finishing buoy was anchored into position twenty-five yards away. We did a set of two races and the Welsh boat came in last-but-one and last. Overall position: last. We were overtaken at one stage by a dead jellyfish.

The Lions moved somewhat faster that night at the WACA, the home of Western Australian cricket. It was a magnificent stadium with stands, like the Lillee and Marsh, named after giants of the summer sport. A fine rain fell on the fastest, bounciest strip in the one game, making it perfect for the studs of another. Floodlights whose output must be visible from outer space illuminated the stage and enhanced the atmosphere. I have always liked night-rugby. The somewhat dimmer lights of Pontypool Park used to shine down on some of our biggest games. When derby rivals like Newport came to play on a Wednesday evening, the sound of ten thousand unseen spectators on the pitch-black bank used to give us an extra buzz. And nights when there was just the first crispy feel of frost on the ground, when clouds of steam would swirl up into the lights, were even more special.

Any sense of gladiatorial confrontation at the warm, wet WACA that night lasted about thirty seconds. That was how long it took the Lions to put in a couple of shuddering tackles and a few thundering runs and announce to the amateurs of this rugby outpost in the far west that they were in for a torrid time. There was still a place for the Lions on tour to do some missionary work, by taking the game to some far-flung spots. But a mismatch was a mismatch anywhere, and care had to be taken not to stifle enthusiasm by exposing it to professional slaughter.

The props Phil Vickery and Darren Morris in particular did the damage. First with their tackling, then with their scrummaging. They seemed to be engaged in some private contest to see who could inflict the more pain.

Almost everybody set off at a gallop. Malcolm O'Kelly did well at the line-out, especially on the opposition throw, Will Greenwood rode tackles and delivered passes and Scott Quinnell made ground with every charge. The number eight scored the first try in the third minute.

Danny Grewcock made the point that not only Malcolm O'Kelly could win ball. He caught a throw at the line-out, the forwards drove on and Robert Howley sold a dummy and ran in for the second try. A third soon followed. Western Australia were turned over, the ball went down the three-quarter line and Dan Luger showed that he was fit to tour. Western Australia tried to reinforce their ranks. Duncan McRae, with his experience in Super 12 and the English Premiership, was not the only ringer on the WA side. They had also been asked to include Patricio Noriega on the bench. At the 1995 World Cup in South Africa the prop had been part of a formidable scrummage, otherwise known as Argentina. The Pumas couldn't help but love the scrum. Everyone else in the world game had spent the previous five years working out ways to reduce the importance of the set-piece, while Argentina kept on coming up with plans to enhance its significance. Noriega had then emigrated to Australia, where he had played for New South Wales, ACT and the Wallabies themselves. Then he went on his travels to Europe, ending up with Stade Français in Paris. Rumour had it that he was back in Australia because the Wallabies, afraid of what might be coming at them in the scrummage in the Test series, had specifically asked him to return.

Unfortunately for Patricio, he did not seem to make that much of a difference. The gulf in class between the Lions and WA grew wider and wider. Within two minutes of his arrival Will Greenwood was on the end of a move that included a break by Brian O'Driscoll. Almost everyone was making an encouraging start to the tour, but it might be overly generous to include Brian in the list. He made that break, but a fullback he wasn't. Nor was Ben Cohen entirely comfortable on the right wing. The harder he tried, the more his timing was out. His frustration was visible; he was playing in a side scoring a try every four and a half minutes and he was missing out.

Neil Back scored two tries in succession from drives after a line-out. This was pure practice for what was to come, we thought. Catch, drive, wriggle. Neil Back the scorer. We might as well enjoy the romps now because in the Tests it was going to be a lot more esoteric. That was what we were thinking in Perth, at any rate.

The romp included a run by Danny Grewcock who, at six feet six inches and seventeen and a half stone, positively gambolled towards the posts. Scott Quinnell scored again – without the gambol. Scott was definitely not a gambolling player, running as he did lower to the ground and being denser of tissue. Dan Luger rather showed the forwards how to do it by high-stepping clear for his second try. At half-time the Lions led 57–0.

Simon Taylor was the first replacement to come off the bench for the second half. The twenty-one-year-old only had four Scottish caps to his name but his athleticism for the Edinburgh Reivers had apparently caught the eye of the assistant Lions coach, Andy Robinson. He came on as a replacement for Richard Hill who had twinged his back. The new wing forward was sensational. He ran in a try from deep and delivered a reverse try-making flip-pass to Iain Balshaw, who also appeared as a replacement. In one short burst Simon Taylor had fully justified his selection.

In all, the Lions scored eighteen tries, with hat-tricks for Scott Quinnell and Dan Luger, braces for Rob Howley, Neil Back and Iain Balshaw, and singles for Will Greenwood, Mark Taylor, Danny Grewcock, Simon Taylor, Austin Healey, who also came on as a replacement, and Brian O'Driscoll. Thirteen of the tries were converted by Ronan O'Gara. The one bad aspect of their play in the second half was that they let in Western Australia for two tries. They were thereby condemned to more defensive drills in training.

It wasn't the only thing to go wrong. Sometime later that Friday night, something went pop in Simon Taylor's knee. The young wing forward, who had just laid out his credentials, asked James Robson, the tour doctor, to have a look at it. Robson felt the knee and shook his head. Taylor's tour was over.

After the press conference, during which everybody had said what you'd expect them to say after a 116–10 victory, Graham Henry was strolling down the perimeter walkway when a group of Lions supporters started to sing him 'Happy Birthday'. And why not? The coach was after all turning fifty-five. The gesture lost its generosity of spirit when someone from the back threw a glass of beer over him. A race was launched to find the culprit. Perhaps not so much to find him or her, but to work out his or her nationality. Welsh or Australian; the bookies couldn't decide which to make favourite. It turned out to be a local Australian male. A small sigh of relief escaped.

I missed the action. I was looking for Austin Healey. It was column time for the *Observer* and it seemed more convenient to have a word with him now, because the next day the caravan would be crossing the country. The Lions would be on one plane, most of the press on another. I knew the players were assembling on the other side of a door at the rear of the media room. But on this door was stuck a notice: 'Strictly No Access.' I nipped through it. No sign of Austin. I nipped back.

Suddenly the Lions captain appeared. Martin Johnson, with that frown to end all frowns, aimed one at me. He jabbed the door. Strictly no access. He jabbed again. Strictly no access.

'What did you want?' he said.

'Austin,' I stammered.

'I'll get him,' said Johnson. It was the sort of thing that made you view players in a new light.

A minute later Austin was coming through he same door. He was wearing just a towel. He looked in great shape.

He was worse than knackered. He'd had an asthma attack the night before and coughed up what he called 'bucketloads of dark green shit'. He'd come on as a sub, but hadn't been able to breathe, hadn't been able to keep up with the action.

He'd still scored a try, a run-in from halfway which included a dummy to set him on his solo way. Eye-catching, but that too had done him in. He said he was ready to leave cold, wet Perth with its days of double-training, and head for the tropical climate of North Queensland and the second chapter of the tour.

6

To the tropics

The Lions were due to fly by charter from Perth to Townsville via Alice Springs. This seemed a direct way of doing things, to go from the bottom left-hand corner of Australia to the top right, straight over the middle, from supposedly Mediterranean Perth to tropical North Queensland. On their flight would be a small group of journalists, apparently approved by the management as a cross-section of the Lions' nationalities.

The rest of the press, meanwhile, were to travel by an altogether more roundabout route, via Melbourne and Brisbane. From bottom left to bottom right and then all the way up the eastern seaboard. For those of us on this scheduled service it meant an early start and the promise of a late arrival in Townsville.

Next to me on the first leg to Melbourne was a large, weather-beaten man called Norm. He had huge hands. He had been raised in northern Victoria on a farm of six thousand acres, of which two thousand could sustain wheat and four thousand remained scrub. His family had lived mostly on kangaroo meat. Fifty years ago when Norm was a boy their house had no electricity. He had left Victoria to go to Queensland to play semi-pro Australian Rules football, and had gone from playing to coaching and then into all sorts of jobs, including selling second-hand cars, running a post office and later a supermarket down in the Margaret River region of Western Australia. He now ran a small delivery-van service in Perth, but had once driven larger trucks across the Nullarbor Plain.

He told of the rare days of rain on that vast tract that stretches across 100,000 square miles of South and Western Australia. The surface of the road is slightly raised above the desert and the water runs off and collects in roadside ditches. The animals of the Nullarbor come to these ditches to drink, so there could be scenes of carnage on the carriageway as wombats, dingoes, possums and kangaroos wandered into the path of any traffic. Truck drivers would invite cars to stick close to their tailgates and would use their indicators to warn of animals ahead. Left indicator for trouble on the left, right for right and both indicators simultaneously for general mayhem. 'Kangaroos are a panel-beater's best friend,' said Norm.

As was the way with journalists, those on the scheduled, roundabout route kept tabs on the chosen few on the charter. Just to make sure nobody had a head-start on any news story. Something strange was going on. First of all, the Lions were still in Perth. A storm had delayed them and then their plane developed a mechanical problem. The party all trooped off to the Burswood Hotel and Casino for some food and roulette. By the time they returned to the airport, Simon Taylor was gone, bound for home and his parents' home in Crieff.

That must have been bizarre for the players. One minute the youngest Lion was in Australia, the next he was in Scotland. No fuss. No goodbyes. Just gone. It wasn't the only odd thing. What was most peculiar was that the journalists now in Melbourne seemed to know more about the Lions than the ones stuck in Perth with them. Word had come through from Canada, where England were on tour, that Martin Corry of Leicester had already been summoned as Simon's replacement.

The Lions management had said nothing. Word then came back that this wasn't quite true either. Graham Henry had confirmed in a BBC radio interview over the telephone with Nicky Campbell, who was in London, that Corry had indeed been sent for. It was another example of the management excluding the press on their doorstep. They appeared to be only

too willing to invite into their camp carefully vetted documen-
tary-makers and agents of the sponsors, who could be guaranteed to produce nothing but puff-pieces, but they were shutting
out a section that might prove more critical.

It was a thorny issue. I remember sitting at the back of a bus in
Cardiff and putting contact with the press to the vote. The Welsh
team of my day did not always, if ever, enjoy happy relations
with a certain section of the Welsh rugby-writers who had been
in the habit of having only tales of glory to report. The great
Welsh era of the 1970s had become an age of painful transition
in the early eighties. After Paul Ringer was sent off in the 1980
game against England, which we lost, rather heroically in our
eyes, 8–9 to Bill Beaumont's Grand Slam England, we felt we
were savaged unfairly. A period of bitter introspection followed.
In the opinion of the players going through that process of losing
as many games as we won, the press was unfair.

Guidelines – no, rules – had been introduced. The media were
allowed to speak only to the chairman of selectors, the captain
and any new caps before international matches. The press had
asked for more. Should we continue with the existing arrangement, or should we make ourselves generally more available?
The vote on the bus in 1983 was unanimous: keep them out.

Looking back, I think it was a mistake. We should have
opened up. Perhaps we would have been treated with greater
tolerance. In my experience as a writer on rugby, once you had
spoken to a player, interviewed him or done a feature on him
you felt more supportive of him. You followed his career with
more interest. You willed him to play well. As captain of Wales
way back, I was the leader who put it to the vote and chose to
exclude the press. We were criticised more than ever.

It was felt before the tour of 2001 that Donal Lenihan would
not be an easy communicator. In the management's defence,
they were busy. There was precious little time to blend a team.
The tour was already one week old. They were working at a
furious rate and yet they had to be circumspect. Australia, in the
new professional age of meticulous research into the opposition,
would be monitoring the Lions' every move.

But that might be to overstate the case for the infiltration of industrial espionage into rugby. We all knew of stories of strangers being found in toolsheds, pretending to be mending the mowers by pointing a video camera at the pitch outside, but in general, people generally respected the difference between an open training session and one behind closed doors. And what were we talking about, anyway? Revealed rugby secrets were hardly going to trigger a crash on Wall Street. If the Lions remained guarded in their release of information, we would not be able to control the formation of a conspiracy theory. So, we formed one. They were going out of their way to be obstructive.

As long as they continued to win by a hundred points, it mattered not a jot how they treated the press. But if the tour ever went pear-shaped, sharpened knives would be poised.

The press pack arrived in Townsville at ten o'clock on Saturday night, unexpectedly four hours ahead of the Lions. I immediately began to look for a television set that showed the cable network Fox Sport.

Stephen Jones and Nick Cain of the *Sunday Times* had rather cunningly rearranged their schedule to take in the Wallabies' warm-up game against the New Zealand Maoris in Sydney. I had what I thought was an equally cunning plan: to watch the re-run of the match on Fox Sport and still file a piece for the *Observer*.

Could I find Fox Sport in Townsville? Nowhere. I ran from bar to bar, from hotel to hotel. All I discovered was that nights in tropical North Queensland were indeed balmier than in Perth. I was dripping wet within seconds.

I ended up watching cricket on Channel 7 in The Australian, a pub near our hotel-apartments. England were losing to Australia in Cardiff in the one-day triangular series that included Pakistan. The sound was turned down because it was karaoke night.

Not surprisingly I slept badly. But beautifully the next morning. I awoke at midday, deemed the weather far too warm for running and set off for a stroll along The Strand, Townsville's own prom. I walked into the Anzac Memorial Park, which commemorated Australia's fallen in war. There was a series of sites in the park; one for example recalling the Battle of the Coral Sea, the naval engagement in 1942 that, despite heavy Allied losses, effectively put an end to the threat of a Japanese invasion of Australia. Gallipoli, of course, was there. And a memorial to the ninety-six Australian servicemen who had been awarded the Victoria Cross.

That night, at Michels restaurant the debate continued about the tensions between the press and the Lions' management. It was generally considered that this was the sort of thing that needed to be nipped in the bud.

We went from Michels to Molly Malone's on Townsville's main drag. Just for a nightcap. In we went and there, sitting in the corner, was Declan Kidney, the successful coach of Munster in Ireland. He was out here watching the Lions and recruiting former Wallaby back-row forward Jim Williams for Munster. 'Evening, Declan,' we all said.

And next to Declan was Donal Lenihan himself. The manager of the Lions. 'Evening, Donal,' we all said. And breezed on past to the bar. As acts of nipping in the bud went, it was about as effective as cutting back nettles by humming at them.

The next day was special. We decided to continue our policy of tackling the sticky issue by ignoring it again. Mick Cleary of the *Daily Telegraph* had persuaded the skipper of a Pure Pleasure Cruise whopping great catamaran to break his habit of not going out to sea on a Monday. If Mick could rustle up a party of about a dozen, the skipper would put a few calls in to the local hotels, and if the numbers formed a quorum of forty, he'd take us to Kelso Reef.

The Great Barrier Reef. It was too enticing to resist. A dozen or so of us duly reported to the quayside to board the catamaran. The skipper had filled his quota. So, off we went, calling first at Magnetic Island, a resort just off Townsville, to pick up more passengers. As we left Magnetic Island behind us, the ocean began to grow. The water turned dark blue and white-topped. The cat ploughed on and on, pitching and rolling through the swell. Paul Morgan turned dark green. He hung on for as long as he could, but with a weak smile he rose to his feet and stuck his green head in a blue bucket.

Two and a half long hours later we entered the shallow waters of the reef. The sea grew calm and dark blue changed to light green. Paul's head came out of the bucket. We spent four hours anchored off Kelso Reef. Some of our crew went scuba diving, but there was no real need to go deep. With a mask and snorkel you could pass within inches of the brilliantly coloured coral and the myriad shoals of fish. As snorklers say, it was breathtaking.

We dived and then we broke for lunch, a magnificent spread of barbecued meat and vegetables, served up by the real crew. And then we dived again. And then we had some more food.

At half past four it was time to leave. One of the instructors offered sea-sickness medication. Paul bought everything she had. The catamaran carefully turned about, we said farewell to Kelso Reef and headed for home.

We hit deep water about twenty minutes later. Having been told that he was less likely to be ill if he had some food, Paul took all of thirty seconds to throw up all his lunch and medication. Back he disappeared into his blue bucket.

The skipper appeared. This was nothing, just a normal swell. He looked at Paul and tapped him with his deck-shoe. 'That's the blue Pacific over there,' he said, 'and you've got your head in a blue bucket. Why don't you chunder in the big bath?'

Another crewman appeared and peered into the bucket. 'Reckon that's a record,' he said and went on his way.

The Lions had announced their team to play against the Queensland President's XV. Now, Queensland was more of a rugby state than Western Australia, but Townsville was more of a rugby league town, home of the North Queensland Cowboys. This game, according to Intelligence, was going to be trickier but would still amount to little more than a warm-up for the real tour, which would begin in four days' time in Brisbane against the Super 12 outfit, the Queensland Reds.

Will Greenwood found himself playing his second game in

four days, although he would be moving across from inside to outside centre to partner Ireland's Rob Henderson. Otherwise, it was all-change. Martin Corry had arrived from Canada and was put straight into the team at number eight. Leicester now had four players on tour: Martin Johnson, Neil Back, Austin Healey and now Martin Corry. This was the same number as Bath, who had sent Mike Catt, Iain Balshaw, Matthew Perry and Danny Grewcock, although the last had yet to play for his new West Country employers. His departure from Saracens meant that the London club could now only boast three: Dan Luger, Richard Hill and Scott Murray. Cardiff also had four on tour: Rob Howley, Neil Jenkins, Martyn Williams and David Young. Swansea, Llanelli and Harlequins all had three for the moment. The figures would change as the injury toll grew, but it would be giving little away to say that Leicester would eventually take the title of club with the most Lions.

Martin Corry wasn't the only newcomer on tour. Back in Fremantle hooker Phil Greening had injured a knee in training. A freak accident, we were told. Out of the blue, Gordon Bulloch of Glasgow Caledonians – their first Lion – and Scotland had been sent for. It was announced that Phil would remain with the party in the hope that he would recover in time for the Tests, but it still meant that the tour was one game old – one warm-up game old – and already two replacements had been winged in. Gordon Bulloch was to sit on the bench.

On either side of Martin Corry of England in the back row were two Welsh wing forwards, Colin Charvis and Martyn Williams. There was quite a Welsh flavour to the side, since the front row contained Robin McBryde at hooker and David Young as captain and tight-head prop. It was the start of a demanding period in the long rugby life of the midweek captain. Tom Smith of Scotland took the spot on the other side of the front row.

Neil Jenkins was at outside half and Dafydd James was on the right wing. It was not known whether Dafydd and Jason Robinson, the other wing, had discussed who would play where. We rather took it for granted that Dafydd would have said that he was willing to play anywhere, left, right, inside, outside, open, blind, front, middle, tight or loose. Once again, there was no Martin Johnson in the second row. Jeremy Davidson had his chance to reiterate why he had been one of the stars of 1997 and Scott Murray had his to show why he was the leading candidate to partner Johnson in the Tests and become one of the stars of 2001. Seldom in the history of rugby had quite so much interest been shown in the heart of the old boilerhouse.

Yapping away at the forwards, and presumably the referee, would be Matt Dawson at scrum half. And behind everyone at fullback was Matt Perry. Brian O'Driscoll was released from the fullback laboratory, the experiment having been declared interesting but not very instructive.

Back out on the Coral Sea, the skipper was doing some instructing of his own. He pointed to an island in the distance. It looked idyllic, with rolling ranges of hills covered in dense vegetation. 'That's Palm Island,' he said. 'It's an Aboriginal reservation. It's the most dangerous place on earth outside a war zone.'

Without wishing to touch upon the sensitivities of Australia's race politics, I wondered if this could be true. If it were, Palm Island must truly be a terrible place. It had to be, to be worse than Johannesburg.

Jo'burg was a frightening city. And if you worked in rugby you tended to find yourself there rather a lot. The last time I was there was in 2000, following the England tour. Before that, in 1998, we had stopped there briefly on our way to the relative safety of Cape Town. I mention that earlier England tour only because it was the Tour from Hell and always triggered the most bizarre memories. This was the tour that took in all three southern hemisphere rugby-playing giants: Australia, New Zealand and South Africa. Such an all-embracing challenge would be arduous enough with a full-strength party. But England coach Clive Woodward had decided to give his senior players, who had all toured with the Lions to South Africa in 1997, a summer off. So he found himself facing four Tests against the world's best with a second-string side.

Their very first game was a Test against Australia, Jonny Wilkinson's debut international. He must have been all of fourteen years old. Or had he just celebrated his nineteenth birthday when he missed all his kicks at goal? Behind the dead-ball line at one end of Suncorp Stadium in Brisbane was a gang of 'push-up boys' who celebrated every point with a series of press-ups to match the total of the side that had just scored. They were too exhausted to move by the end of the game. England lost 0–76.

From there they went immediately to New Zealand, where they lost two Tests in Dunedin and Auckland. Danny Grewcock was sent off. Clive Woodward had a row with John Hart when he caught the All Black coach trying to enter the referee's room at half-time. It was a strange time for Clive. He then had to fly back to England for the funeral of his father. He rejoined the team and went with them from Auckland to Cape Town via Hong Kong and Johannesburg. Hence, the Tour from Hell.

In Cape Town the England coach had his most wonderfully brilliant wacky moment. The team were staying in an average hotel next door to the Newlands stadium. One day the South African Under-21 squad arrived and took up residence in the same hotel. Now, Clive's team were 0–3 down in Tests. They were the laughing stock of the southern hemisphere, although they had actually regrouped after Brisbane and were going down valiantly, if nothing else. They had also scandalised the powers that be, in Australia especially, by daring to send out a sub-standard squad. It was insulting, according to the Australian chief executive, John O'Neill.

So, one way or another, Clive was under a fair bit of strain. And then he saw this Springbok development team in the same hotel as his England boys. He called his team together, told them to pack their bags immediately, marched them across town to the best hotel in Africa, the Mount Nelson, and ordered twenty rooms on his own credit card. Pure class. If ever he proved that he had the vision to lead England into a new age of daring, it was there and then.

To move on, though, to the tour of 2000, with England in

Johannesburg. It was on this tour that Clive's England did make the quantum leap into adventure. They left Jo'burg for the day to play the second Test in Bloemfontein, having lost the first in Pretoria, and finally unleashed the fluid handling game that would stun the Six Nations Championship the following year.

The point, though, was that Johannesburg was a hairy place. Its murder count was off the chart. You had to be very careful to take local advice about where you went and when. Or did you? Stuart Barnes, the former England outside half and now Sky Sport's summariser, had a theory. Over dinner one night in the confines of Sandton, one of the city's hermetically sealed safety zones, he argued that if we were true to our non-racist beliefs we should not be here in the white man's fortress, but braving the shebeens of Soweto. Fine, Barnsey, was the riposte. But there was a reality to Johannesburg, which was called surviving. The argument went on.

The next day Stuart stepped out of the Sandton bubble. A taxi driver ran past him, hotly pursued by another. The second man took out a gun and calmly shot the first. Stuart did an about-turn and ran back into his fortress. He was not seen for three days.

One of the safest places in South Africa was the golf course. Or the golf resort as they were offered in the brochures, offering sport and security. This was the excuse Ian Robertson and I had been looking for. It would be irresponsible to expose our lives to unnecessary danger by not playing. So, we were responsible at every opportunity. As we were driving to Sun City one morning we were stopped at a police roadblock. For some strange reason I was on the phone at the time, having been called by my bank manager to discuss the overdraft. The usual thing. The bank manager had to listen as the policeman explained that we could go no further because there had been a serious incident just over there. A robbery and a shooting. If you looked carefully, sirs, you could see the blood. The bank manager said he'd phone back later. I don't think we had our best round that day.

We passed Palm Island and returned to Townsville at eight o'clock. At midnight it still felt as though we were on the Pure Pleasure Cruise.

The next day was Tuesday and in the evening the Lions would play their second game, against the Queensland President's XV. That left the morning free for, of all things, golf. Twenty-four of us pitched up at the Willows Club and frightened the life out of the pro there who said he couldn't cope and sent us on our way to Rowes Bay GC. Such a dismissal would never happen in South Africa.

At Rowes Bay we split up into teams of three. I was playing with David Hands of *The Times* and Chris Hewett of the *Independent*. The weather was gorgeous and the course welcoming. We were interrupted on the tee by wild marsupials. It was all great fun. We finished last but one.

That night eighteen and a half thousand people came to the home of the North Queensland Cowboys rugby league team. The target figure was twenty thousand, and the number was important because Townsville was trying to persuade the Queensland rugby union authorities to let them host a Super 12 game. The Queensland Reds might one day play at the Dairy Farmers Stadium. Who said there was no romance in a place-name? They laid on quite a party at the Dairy Farmers, with fireworks and a host presenter in a loud jacket who filled the big screen with small talk. The Beatnix provided the live music and for forty minutes the Queensland President's XV did the cabaret.

The Lions' line-out did not work. Hooker Robin McBryde went off with a dead leg after nine minutes. Treatment to his haematoma probably prevented him from watching as Jeremy Davidson did the most hurtful thing and won a line-out. The forwards drove and Dai Young scored.

Ten minutes later the Lions scored again, but it nearly cost them the head of Matt Perry. The fullback was smashed by a tackle from President's centre Junior Pelesasa which looked high and deadly. Referee George Ayoub let it go. Or perhaps he was just playing advantage. Perhaps he was interested to see what Jason Robinson could do. He had already seen the little winger prevent a try by wriggling under opposition fullback Nathan Williams on the Lions' tryline. And he had penalised him a

couple of times for not releasing in the tackle. It was worth not
blowing on this occasion. Jason was off, his dancing, darting
running making you twitch in your seat. He did not make for
comfortable viewing. From the ruck he set up, the ball came to
Colin Charvis who showed a fine turn of pace of his own. The
Lions had scored their second try. And it was a mighty relief to
see Matt Perry alive and well. He had been hit a hammer-blow to
his chest area but he was able to shrug it off. Rugby injuries are
an enigma of science. A high-velocity collision can be shrugged
off one day, while the next an innocuous challenge can end a
career.

The Lions then stopped functioning. The whole team now
made for uncomfortable viewing. They were all trying too hard
to force the game. Eighteen tries in the opening game had set a
benchmark, and the new team were too anxious to be on their
way towards a similar goal of a hundred points. Seasoned,
quality players were looking out of sorts. Matt Dawson and
Neil Jenkins were throwing the ball into a lot of dead space. The
opposition cabaret struck up once again. Jason Robinson was
not allowed to celebrate his contribution to Charvis's try for
long. Wing forward Scott Fava picked him up the next time he
tried to burst into midfield and dumped him unceremoniously in
a heap.

Outside half Shane Drahm kicked two penalties to reduce the
gap to four points. The President's team then defended their line
to deny the Lions a pair of tries as the first half drew to a close.
When George Ayoub blew for the interval there was wild
applause for the home side. At half-time the tourists led only
10–6.

At the interval the players sat down in the changing room and
sorted it out for themselves. During the first half a curt message
had been relayed from the coaches, via the head-set of the water-
carrier Lawrence Dallaglio, to the players that they should stop
playing as individuals and start playing as a team. The message
had not been absorbed. Now in the changing room it was an
important moment for the tour, a mini-crisis. Nobody screamed
or shouted. They worked it out.

In the second half they scored seventy-three uninterrupted points. Colin Charvis started the ball rolling with his second try, scored immediately after the restart. Martyn Williams stole a ball in loose play for a turnover that led to Jason Robinson's first try in a Lions shirt. Scott Murray with a catch set up a twenty-metre drive from a line-out that ended with a penalty try. The forwards tossed a Queensland President's scrum into reverse to release Rob Henderson for the first of his solo tries. Martin Corry combined with Matt Dawson for Robinson's second try. The wing then looked out of the ruck he had set up to see Rob Henderson's second solo effort, which concluded with a little kick and chase to the line. Austin Healey came off the bench and combined with Henderson, Dafydd James and Jason Robinson again for Robinson's third try. Jason Leonard deftly put Malcolm O'Kelly over with a pass. The tall second row enjoyed his gallop to the posts. Jason Robinson then ran in his fourth and fifth tries before Rob Henderson brought the evening to a close with his third.

The final score was 83–6. The driving line-out had again played second-fiddle to expansion and adventure. Jason Robinson had crossed five times, which wasn't quite a Lions record since David Duckham, against West Coast/Buller on the 1971 tour of New Zealand, and J.J. Williams, against South Western Districts in South Africa in 1974, had each scored six. But as a debut performance it wasn't bad. There might be a few strains on the communication front off the field, but not apparently between the players on it. They had run into difficulties, had remained calm and had run their way out of trouble. The first two outings had only been warm-up games but the Lions were averaging 99.5 points per game, which put them up there with Don Bradman.

That night the team went into town for a few beers. But not by themselves. Fans were now everywhere. Only a few had been in Perth; now their numbers were swelling. The Lions ended up in an autograph signing session.

The supporters were an essential part of the touring process. They provided wonderful support. But they could be wearing. I, too, met one that night. 'You don't know me, but I know you,' said the very first one I ran into. 'I'm from Lancashire and I disagree with just about everything you have to say on the game.'

It could have been worse. It certainly was for a couple of the opposition players. Not all the President's men managed to find their way to bed early. Some were out to enjoy themselves, including Nathan Williams and Shane Drahm who were in the Queensland Reds squad due to play against the Lions in the very next fixture. As the pair returned to their hotel they were slightly unfortunate to bump into Mark McBain, the coach of the Reds, who was waiting at a taxi rank, on his way to the airport for an early flight. Nathan and Shane were summarily dropped from the Reds.

7

Brisbane first-time round

The following morning we left Townsville for Brisbane. Our flight was not quite as early as Mark McBain's but it was still at a disagreeable hour. At a coffee-bar in Departures I bumped into John Rutherford, who had been a Lions selector and had been invited out to Australia to watch and absorb for a week. John was part-time backs coach to the Scottish team. He knew he really should be doing it full-time. 'Rugby is in my blood,' he said. A few years previously, however, he had set up an insurance business with a couple of mates and he did not want to let them down.

This was not John's first Lions tour. He, like myself, had been on the '83 trip to New Zealand. Unlike me he had been very much a first-choice tourist, a consummate outside half who formed a record-breaking Scottish half-back partnership with Roy Laidlaw. For the final Test, in order that the selectors might accommodate both himself and Ireland's Ollie Campbell, two rare success stories of the tour, he ended up in the centre.

We sat and sprayed frothy milk over ourselves as we remembered the good old days. In 1983 Steve Boyle of England had gone as one of the second rows but was having a lot of trouble getting a game, let alone mounting a challenge for a Test place. Steve was known as 'Foggy', short for Foghorn. He was a big bloke with a booming voice. After six weeks, which in those days amounted to about half the tour, he decided to challenge management on the issue. 'Is there any chance,' he asked Willie John McBride, the manager and former second-row player who, conversely, had once set all sorts of records for the number of games – seventy-one – he had played on five Lions tours, 'that you might be able to let me know if there is the slightest possibility of me actually playing one day?'

'No,' said Willie John.

And that was that. So, there then began an alternative tour around New Zealand. It was called Foggy's Tours and every day a schedule would be pinned on the hotel noticeboard to let everyone know what Steve had planned for himself and any other players likewise deemed surplus to requirements. I became an honorary member for the last few days. His finest moment came at breakfast one morning when he came tripping down the stairs and made a presentation of a pair of dark glasses and a white stick to Jim Telfer.

Only a few journalists travelled to Brisbane. Most had rescheduled their flights to take in the announcement of the team to play in the first real trial of strength, the Saturday-night game at Ballymore against the Queensland Reds. The preamble was over; no more missionary work in cricket stadia in Perth, or rugby league strongholds in Townsville. The Lions were heading for Ballymore, a rugby union fortress whose landlords, the Reds, were a genuine force. Although they had lost five of their first six games in the 2001 Super 12 they had then made a charge towards qualification for the semi-finals by winning five matches on the trot. They had beaten the New South Wales Waratahs in the last round, before losing – rather nastily, it had be said – 6–30 to the ACT Brumbies in their semi-final in Canberra. They might not have played together for a month, and they might be missing the services of three major Wallaby players, John Eales, Ben Tune and Chris Latham, but they had still made the final four of the Super 12. And it was impossible to do that without being a bit tasty.

The announcement of the Lions team to face that lot was a big occasion. And a supplementary morsel had been thrown to the press. They would have access to all the players afterwards. It just so happened that in a similar display of *glasnost* the previous day, we had all been invited to a training session. But most of us then were on the Barrier Reef. It was a question of priorities: snorkling before scrummaging. I don't suppose the management were overwhelmed by our enthusiasm. We had flocked to the open session in the shape of a single representative, Steve Bale. Our lone envoy had reported back, by the way, that Phil Larder's defensive sessions were intriguing. By then we were too queasy to care.

That couldn't have gone down too well on the management side. And when everything ran late the following day and the 'open access' to the players became a scrambled thirty seconds on the run with a handpicked few, it didn't go down too well on ours.

We all met up again in Brisbane. This time we were staying in the same hotel as the players. Would there be a High Noon at the Sheraton?

The Queensland Reds, of course, invited all and sundry to their training. Their president was Paul McLean, the former Wallaby outside half. I remembered a drop goal of his against us at Pontypool. He caught the ball facing the wrong way, about twenty metres from our tryline. He half turned, let go of the ball and flicked his ankle. The ball made contact with the outside of his boot and popped over. Perhaps you had to be there to appreciate it fully. Still . . .

The latest generation of Queenslanders were going through their paces at, um, walking pace. Literally. Through their moves they went without a bead of perspiration appearing on a single brow. In terms of marrying the way you trained with the way you played, it certainly contrasted with what the Lions were allegedly up to.

After their run- . . . no, walk-out, the Reds made themselves available for interviews. Anyone who wished could chat for as long as she or he wished with John Eales, the captain of the Wallabies and a living legend who had won everything in the game, including two World Cup winners' medals in 1991 and

1999. He had even managed to play against Martin Johnson at a level below the superheroic. As tender young things they had met in a New Zealand–Australia fixture at Development level. John was of course Australian, while Martin was in King Country, home province of Colin Meads, on a life-experience sojourn. It was probably where he learnt to crush ribs. Colin 'Pine Tree' Meads, who faced the Lions in eleven Tests, was not one of the more namby-pamby players in the history of rugby.

A decade or so after facing Martin the cub, the only thing left for the star second row of the Wallabies to achieve in rugby was to play against the grown-up Lion. And, of course, recover from the flaring of a chronic Achilles tendon injury, an inflammation that was to keep him out of Saturday's game.

Meanwhile, I was down in the Botanic Gardens off Alice Street. I must confess I found it practically impossible to drag myself to training sessions. I know that I should be more curious about modern drills and zonal cone-work, but I have no ambitions to coach. And I have been through enough of the damned things to know that, however good a batsman looks in the nets, it is only on his performances out in the middle that he can be judged.

So there I was, not at the Reds' training, but down in the Botanic Gardens opposite the Quay West. The gardens were my favourite spot in the whole of Australia and the hotel one of my favourites in the whole world. England had had a nightmare on their Tour from Hell in 1998 and couldn't wait to be on their way from Oz; I had been in the Quay West and could have stayed there for ever.

The Gardens sit on the curve of the Brisbane River in the city-centre, a haven of lawn and arboretum, mango grove and bamboo forest between the water and the high-rises. I was drawn to the shade of the banyan tree. And the peepul, a giant fig tree from India, which strangled the host over which it sprawled in the wild, and yet which remained a source of spiritual inspiration for Buddhists. Or was it Hindus? Anyway, it was a mother of a tree.

It must have worked. I was about to have a mystical moment. I was in the bar with Alastair Hignell when over came Graham Henry. Had we seen Queensland train, he asked. Alastair said he had. And added that he had been able to speak to as many of their players as he wanted afterwards.

'Fancy that,' I said. 'All those players available just like that . . .'

Henry paused. 'Is there a problem? I thought it was going ten out of ten for you guys.'

Before I knew it I was telling the coach of the rising feeling of exclusion among the press corps.

'This must be sorted,' he said.

Later that same night, as we sat in the bar, Andy Robinson, the assistant coach, came over and sat down. As a player Andy had been an open-side wing forward, a fixture in the Bath back row. He had glittered briefly for England at the end of the 1980s, had toured with the Lions of 1989 and had enjoyed a single comeback outing for England against South Africa in 1995. And he had been singled out in our conspiracy as the one most likely to wish the press to be kept at arm's length. Before Clive Woodward had been anointed England manager, and before his own elevation to the post of national coach, Robbo had been director of rugby at Bath. And although Bath under his steward-ship had eventually recovered their position as one of the grand clubs of the British game, they had been through a difficult spell. On many a cold, post-match Saturday afternoon in the season of 1999 he had had to face a hostile press who wanted to know why his champions of Europe were in a slump. When was he going to resign? He handled it well, took all the knocks on the chin and coached Bath back to eminence. But it must have rankled.

Now he joined us at the bar. He was affability itself and talked with informal ease about the progress of the players. He didn't deliver the crown jewels, but there was no need. Simply to have half an hour of his company meant that a bridge had been rebuilt.

Two seats away, Alex Broun was telling Andrew Baldock of the Press Association a different story. Alex was an Australian, a former actor who had once necked Kylie Minogue in *Neighbours*. He had gone on to become media liaison officer with the Springboks in South Africa, which may not appear much of a promotion. But according to a straw poll among journalists he was the best press go-between in the business. With the Springboks, however, he had had a few sharp exchanges with managers of incoming tours, namely the Irish. Namely Donal Lenihan in a previous incarnation.

Alex was now media liaison officer with the Lions. Presumably the hatchet had been buried, although by the way he was bemoaning his situation to Andrew – the impossibility of his job as conduit between the management that were hardly forthcoming and the press on an amber alert of agitation – it seemed that someone had buried it in his head.

The next day the management received a deputation of senior journalists: Peter Jackson of the *Daily Mail*, David Hands of *The Times* and Stephen Jones of the *Sunday Times*. Problems were thrashed out. Schedules would be published, players made more available and training on certain days opened up. Our lot were happier; Alex was happier.

And that night, the eve of the big game against the Queensland Reds, Donal Lenihan came over with Pat O'Keefe, baggage master and fellow Munsterman, and sat down. I bought him a beer; he bought me a beer and we talked. I told him that such informal contacts would iron out any wrinkles of communication. He said they had been so busy that they had not had time for anything. We went back into the old days. Donal had seen me running that morning and had had a laugh at that, all right. He didn't jog himself, thanks to a hip that might need replacing in a few years. It was all so entertaining that Pat was asleep within minutes.

I wasn't sure how important relations with the press were on a Lions tour. Gerry Thornley of the *Irish Times* and I had a chat later and wondered whether we weren't all being a wee bit precious. But an awful lot of words were being sent back every day by an ever-growing army of writers. By the time of the Test series there would be about fifty of us. There did seem to be a hunger back home – and even in France – for news of what was going on, especially since the Lions were growing and growing as a force for good in a summer of general British sporting misery.

We had our own little role after all. But nothing compared with the players'. They, too, could moan. In fact it would have been a strange tour if they hadn't moaned. Even if it was only about the way their pants were ironed. But if anyone had a right to be ever so slightly precious it was the thoroughbred performers who had to go out and risk being battered and abused. And the thing was, they weren't precious. They were top international performers who all knew the score about the hardships of touring. But genuine trouble was brewing. On the Thursday, even as the peace negotiations were going on between press and management, I spoke to Austin about his column for the Friday *Guardian*.

He ripped into the tour, the training and the coaches. He said there was mutiny in the air. He said that all the floggings in training, the sheer volume of work amounted to nothing more than coaching for coaching's sake. He said that the England players who had once had a go at Clive Woodward would never have another bad word said about him. England sessions were light years ahead of what they were going through here. He said that the secret Test plan they were working on would not win the series. If they weren't prepared to maximise the skills of the likes of Iain Balshaw, then the plan was doomed. Mark his words.

He told me not to put that last bit in, about the secret file. And off he went to his room, a decidedly unhappy tourist. He was on the bench again for the third time in three games. He thought he had been carded to start as scrum half against Queensland, but the selectors had opted instead for Rob Howley. Austin had been told he would be playing the following Tuesday against Australia A in Gosford.

It was great stuff. I went upstairs and put it all down. Player mutiny, coaching for coaching's sake; the lot, minus the Test plan. And I filed it.

And then I started to worry. Austin had said that they had had no feedback of the press back home. But this was opinion that would raise a few eyebrows, and if it came bouncing back to Australia, quite a few hackles. It was Austin's own column and could land him in trouble.

The great thing about working on the eastern seaboard of Australia was that you had a time difference of nine hours in your favour. I went out for dinner and fretted for a couple of them. When I went back to the Sheraton I phoned the *Guardian* sports desk and told them I wanted to amend the piece. Ben Clissitt, the sports editor, hesitated and said that would be a shame. He paused again and said that he understood.

I took out the collective feeling of mutiny. I took out the swing at Graham Henry. I left Austin himself feeling worn out and frustrated. I felt better and thought we could get away with that. I went downstairs and who should come in through the doors but Austin himself. He had always said that he wouldn't mind seeing a copy of the column before publication, but I really hadn't gone to any great lengths – well, none at all, really – to comply. I had told him not to worry. I'd tell him before I sank him. I suppose I was still a bit worried. I told him I'd like him to see the piece.

So, up we went to read it. I showed him what I'd written originally and how I'd amended it. He went a bit pale. He asked me to remove any mention of mutiny. He'd calmed down and wasn't fuming at all now. I do believe he thanked me for altering the original. I was relieved too, but wondered how this would affect the relationship between player and ghost-writer thereafter.

I went back down to the Botanic Gardens the next day, back to the peepul tree. Maybe there was a little extraterrestrial tingle in that place, but really I was there for something more ornithological than spiritual. I was involved in a Radio 4 documentary on the tour. Four of the Lions party – Rob Howley, Matt Dawson, Malcolm O'Kelly and fitness adviser Steve Black – had been given mini-discs and we were all putting down thoughts here and there as we went along.

I thought the Gardens would be a good place for a few seconds of build-up to Ballymore, if only because, on the day before, the trees around the pond by the main entrance had been filled with the cries of ibises. They had been making a sound that said, 'This is not Battersea Park. This is the other side of the world.'

But today the ibises, rotund white waddling creatures with ridiculously long black bills, were nowhere to be seen. Still, there seemed to be plenty of subtropical birdsong all around me, so I pressed the record button and said something about Brisbane and Ballymore and the ibises of the Botanic Gardens. When I listened to the tape later, all that could be heard was my voice and the quacks of a few ducks. It did sound like Battersea Park.

The Lions to face the Queensland Reds had to be something near a full-strength Test team. Graham Henry of course said it wasn't. There was a major game to be played the following Tuesday, he reminded us, at Gosford, against Australia A. We could start to interpret things, he allowed, at the time of the announcement of the team to play the New South Wales Waratahs in Sydney on the Saturday after Gosford.

But we couldn't help sifting through the tea-leaves of the team to face the first real challenge of the tour. Tom Smith had been even quieter than usual in Townsville. Darren Morris, by popular consensus, was way ahead in the race of the loose-heads. Tom was selected to play at Ballymore. This had to be a chance for him to make amends. The rest of the pack looked ready-made for Test rugby: Keith Wood at hooker, Phil Vickery on the tight-head, the English second-row pairing of Martin Johnson and Danny Grewcock, and a back row of Neil Back, Richard Hill and Scott Quinnell. Except that Scott was suddenly fat of knee and his place was taken by Martin Corry. Lawrence Dallaglio was still not available for selection.

The halfbacks were Robert Howley and Jonny Wilkinson. The centres were Rob Henderson – a reward for his glittering display in Townsville – and Brian O'Driscoll, now back in the safety of his outside centre berth. Dan Luger was on the left wing, Dafydd James on the right and Iain Balshaw at fullback. If that wasn't as close, we thought, to the Test team as made no difference, then Graham Henry was a stand-up comedian in an Auckland drag-club.

I went for a haircut. I recognise that this was possibly not one of the defining moments of the tour, or even an experience to compare with the lure of the peepul tree. But having a trim in a distant land was a recognition that you were away from home for a long time. On an away-break in Pembrokeshire you didn't waste time having a haircut.

I remember the first haircut I had in Spain. I was living there because Cambridge had offered me a place to read Modern Languages. Since I only had French at A-level they had told me to take a gap year and learn Spanish. I had raced as fast as I could to O-level standard and then, at the age of eighteen, found myself in Madrid with twelve months to kill. I wasn't exactly terrified but I spent the first couple of months in a state of acute loneliness, floundering in a country where I understood barely a word of what was being said. It was a strange place and a strange time, for these were the dying days of the age of Francisco Franco, the dictator who had ruled the country since the end of the Spanish Civil War in 1939.

In September 1975, when I arrived, Franco only just had the strength to make a last, feeble appearance on the balcony of the Palacio del Oriente. Soon he would be on a life-support system that would keep him going until the mechanisms to transfer Spain from dictatorship to a restored order of democratic monarchy were in place.

There I was, lost and lonely in a land that was on the cusp of a new era. It was rugby that handed me a lifeline. I went into a bar on the Calle Gaztambide one evening for a bite to eat. Hanging on the wall were photographs of a rugby team in blue and black shirts. I did not know that they even played rugby in Spain. I had been to see Real Madrid beat Derby County at the Bernabeu Stadium, but rugby struck me as very non-Spanish.

No, no, said the barman. This was the former headquarters of the Industrial Engineers of Madrid, and if I was interested he could give me the number of the current captain. A week later I was a signed-up player of the club, a proud member of the team that was middling to bottom of Castillian Regional Division 3.

It was the start of an unforgettable stay among some of the kindest people on earth. Soon I had the confidence to go for my first haircut.

The only other time I have dipped a toe in the affairs of dictators – if we can discount the reign of Maggie or one of my former dentists – was to do with Romania. In 1983 I was captain of the Welsh team that went to play in Bucharest. And lost, thank you for asking. These were the days of Nicolae Ceauşescu at his maddest. He had gone from being the independently-minded communist leader courted by the West to the barking-mad tyrant who was ripping apart the countryside in order to convert Romania into an industrial powerhouse.

Such a transformation didn't seem to us to be going too well. Life in the capital appeared to be one long queue for bread. Don't speak to anyone was the only advice we were given. Informants were everywhere. Trust no one. Who would have thought Romania shared so much in common with the Welsh Rugby Union?

Six years later Romania rose up, unseated Ceauşescu and put him on trial. His wife, Elena, and he were then put up against a wall and shot. This, give or take a few last murderous bursts from the secret police, the Securitate, brought to an end the Romanian Revolution.

Unfortunately, while the battles raged between Christmas 1989 and the New Year of 1990, one of the players who had starred against us in 1983, Florica Murariu, was killed. Florica played for the army side, Steaua, and had been a key member of the Romanian pack that defied the trend to defect at the first opportunity and stayed together to become gnarled and seriously efficient. They had turned us over quite ruthlessly. He was caught in crossfire while walking home, having been celebrating victory and freedom with some friends.

I was sent out to do an obituary on the late wing forward by

the late *Sunday Correspondent* newspaper. I arrived in Bucharest as the capital was still smouldering and was invited to attend
the first committee meeting of the new Romanian Rugby Fed-
eration. The new officers of the FRR spent the time writing
letters of condolence to the families of the dozen or so rugby
players who had lost their lives.

   At lunchtime I went back to my hotel room, which came
complete with bullet-holes in the window, and turned on the
television. The station was showing pictures of bodies in a
morgue. A single camera panned over the corpses and a quiet
voice identified them wherever possible. A young mother held a
child in her arms, both their faces pockmarked with bullet-holes.
The bottom of a soldier's greatcoat came into view and the
camera rose up his body. 'Murariu, Florica,' said the voice.

I went back to Romania in March 2001, even as I was planning
my trip to Australia with the Lions. Poverty and corruption had
seized rugby there. A hard core of enthusiasts was doing all it
could, ferrying in children from the shanty-town suburbs of
Bucharest to clubs like Dinamo to give them a grounding, but
this was rugby surviving on the tundra. The boots were all hand-
me-downs, the pitches rutted and stony, the coaching barely
elementary. The committee of 1990, when they raised their
glasses to their martyrs and their future, were praying for better
than this.

Quite what all this had to do with the Lions against the Queensland Reds was beyond me. But you couldn't prevent the flow of
memories, as they said in India under the peepul tree, where big
figs grew.

   But the present was very much back on the agenda now. The
following night the Lions played their third match, which
promised to be their first trial of strength. Ballymore sat beneath
blazing floodlights. Smoke and scents from a hundred barbecues
swirled into the bright night air. From tented hospitality to
swilling a cold one out the back, eighteen and a half thousand
people were intent on enjoying their Saturday night at the ball

park. This was a ground that had built its rugby traditions and aimed to preserve them. And yet, the atmosphere was convivial, rather than passionate. Southern hemisphere crowds, with the possible exception of Ellis Park, Johannesburg for the World Cup Final of 1995, were not in the habit of generating the same ferocious sound as the supporters who went to the Six Nations.

South Africa might claim that occasion at Ellis Park, when they beat New Zealand to win the third World Cup, as the day to end all rugby days. New Zealand would say that Carisbrook, the home of Otago in the university city of Dunedin, was the wildest place on big-match day. Australia held the world record for a crowd – 107,042 – set when the Wallabies played the All Blacks at Stadium Australia in 1999, the year before the Sydney Olympics. But nowhere did the crowd produce the sustained ear-splitting decibels of the Six Nations.

It would be wrong to say that in Australia's case the lack of unbridled fervour had anything to do with the type of people who pitched up to rugby union games. These might be largely well-heeled folk, who played the game through the private education system, but restraint and class did not go together here quite as easily as an English chap and his stiff upper lip. Australians liked the banter, as far as I could tell. From Perth to Townsville to Ballymore, it seemed that once you'd given it a rip with the vocals to announce to your team that you were in your seat, then you were quite happy to wait until something happened before shouting again. And in the meantime, if any wag had anything half-witty to say, then all the better if such a bloke was given a bit of hush, so that everybody could hear him, mate. The humour was mostly limited to the usual Pom-bashing stuff, but everyone was prepared to wait patiently for the line that raised a chuckle.

This evening Ballymore had another reason to keep quiet. The Lions tore the Reds apart in a first-half display that sent shock waves around the ground. They had to survive an aggressive start by the home team, a start that included a punch by hooker Michael Foley on Rob Howley and a penalty to put the Reds in the lead. But they came through their ordeal by fire, partly by returning like with like. Phil Vickery had a lecture so long from referee Stuart Dickinson that it became a Baptist sermon. The prop had climbed into a maul with no real care for what he was crushing beneath his studs and was probably only spared a stint in the sin-bin because he was not alone. Everybody was dishing out some pretty meaty treatment whenever a tackle was made. And ferocious tackles were coming thick and fast.

For a time the Lions were under real pressure. They tried to move the ball wide, but when Brian O'Driscoll received it he was buried beneath a defence screaming up to nail him. It was a mean-spirited opening ten-minute period, and very absorbing.

Martin Johnson, having donned a playing shirt for the first time on tour, gave the Lions shape. By knocking the Reds out of shape. He put in a shuddering tackle that spilt the ball his team's way. It reached Dafydd James on the right wing, who made a good run. The defence closed him down but he recycled the ball at a ruck. Neil Back stood in at scrum half and dive-passed to Jonny Wilkinson. The outside half looked up for an instant and laser-guided a kick the width of the field for Dan Luger to score on the left wing.

Another kick by Wilkinson, this time straight downfield, nearly created a try for Iain Balshaw. At least the Lions ended up on the Reds' line, and when they earned themselves a penalty, their outside half could perfect the other side of his kicking game. He had missed with the conversion, but he would not miss another place-kick all night.

Having clicked into gear and begun to play with control and power, the Lions then scored a riot of a try. It began elegantly enough with a steal by Richard Hill on the Queensland throw. But things broke down when Balshaw lost the ball in the tackle. Queensland then lost it in their turn. There was only one thing to do with this bar of soap: give it some old Irish imperial leather. Rob Henderson and Keith Wood hacked at the ball and charged after it. The old foot-rush. Kick ahead Ireland; any feckin' head. Henderson at the end restored elegance by scooping the ball up for the try.

The kicking game was working a treat. The Reds were rushing

up, and the Lions were rushing them back with kicks – of all descriptions – behind them. We had seen the precision crossfield punt, then the Irish hack. And now we were about to witness the delicate chip, as demonstrated by that old master of the subtle touch, Keith Wood. The only time a hooker would put a foot on a ball in the old days was by sliding the end of his leg under his chin, three inches off the ground, and scraping it back through the scrum. Now, they could express themselves in open play as long as they had the skill to do it. Your man Woody did.

The build-up to his moment of gracefulness was not a thing of grace. Martin Corry, who was having quite the most outstanding game, put in a tackle of Johnsonesque proportions on Matt Cockbain and made a right mess of the Wallaby Test player. This must not only have upset the back-rower *per se* but must also have been a blow to his sense of general good order. Apparently Matt is obsessively neat and tidy. In his wardrobe, ironed shirts have to be arranged in strict order of colour on equidistantly spaced hangers. He loves tidying away clothes, towels and toys, putting the bins out and mowing the lawn. Ah, the lawn. A kindred spirit. There is a lot to be said for lawn management, although for the moment Matt was in a bit of a mess on the Ballymore turf beneath Corry's tackle. In such a heap, in fact, that the ball once again was turned over in favour of the Lions. Keith Wood received it and dinked it behind his opposite number Michael Foley. The hooker turned but he knew the game was up. Hooker turning did not beat winger chasing. Dafydd James flew past him to score.

There was more to come. The Lions put together a series of rucks, but without the crispness that might spell trouble for a well-organised defence. The Reds duly kept them out and the ball was dragged back equally slowly from the next breakdown. Although the Lions were quite near the line their progress looked too ponderous to carry menace. One inside pass from Jonny Wilkinson to Richard Hill, however, and the well-organised defence was split asunder. The wing forward was through and over. The Lions at half-time led – and here we all rubbed our eyes – 32–3. It had been a sublime last thirty minutes.

Only one player had failed to live up to his billing. Nothing had really happened for Brian O'Driscoll. He had been well contained by an opposition midfield containing two Wallabies, Elton Flatley and Daniel Herbert, and inside centre Steve Kefu. Brian might have been a bit wary of gliding too wide in case he ran into the battering-ram body of winger Junior Pelesasa, the player who had nearly drilled a hole the size of a cardboard cut-out of himself in the chest of Matt Perry in Townsville.

Whatever. Brian had been quiet in the first half. In the fourth minute of the second half he burst into life. Jonny Wilkinson made a half-break and his outside centre made it whole. O'Driscoll timed his run and his angle to perfection, took a short pass and blazed through. Sustained gas and sure balance took him to the line. Wilkinson added his fifth conversion and then his second penalty. The Lions led 42–3. Stunning.

They then stopped again. It was almost as if they realised what they were doing, embarrassing a side that had gone to the semi-finals of the Super 12. It was a bit, er, embarrassing to be doing that. Or perhaps they took rather too seriously their brief to reveal as little as possible to watching Wallaby eyes about their strategy for the Tests. Perhaps they simply grew tired.

They certainly let their level of performance drop, and since this was to last a full twenty minutes, it meant that the brilliance of an hour rather lost its gloss. Matt Dawson had a kick charged down by his opposite number Sam Cordingley who was only a yard and a half offside, and the Reds had the satisfaction of scoring the final try of the game.

Still, it had been for a time the most exceptional performance. By the team and by most individuals. Martin Johnson had arrived at last on the playing field. His presence had been felt. Danny Grewcock had shown that he could spoil ball on the opposition throw, which put him ahead in the race for the second-row spot alongside the captain. Richard Hill was just as constructive and destructive in the back row. Rob Henderson had made a big claim on the inside-centre jersey. Jonny Wilkinson had run the show with aplomb, astounding the Australians who only remembered him as the eighteen-year-old overwhelmed by his first taste of international football back in Brisbane in 1998.

The real man of the match was Martin Corry, the replacement number eight for Simon Taylor. He was enormous in the tackle whether advancing or covering back. He sorted out the scrummages that wheeled and he linked well with the ball in his hands in open play. The coach at the press conference afterwards was delighted to see someone so determined to show him he had been wrong not to select him in the first place. Corry simply said that he too was delighted, but that he had to be at the top of his game even to survive in the company of the guys all around him in the squad. It was another bonus, another hand raised for selection in the Test team.

The downside was that the scrum creaked a bit. And the Lions had only won the second half 10–5, the final score being 42–8.

To celebrate what we in the stands all wanted to call majestic and inspiring, a real watershed moment, a crossroads crossed, a test passed, Martin Johnson said it had been nothing more than satisfactory. Graham Henry thought that, overall, the Lions had been fortunate to have the bounce of the ball in the first half. He didn't like the second. There was so much more work to do.

But at least we knew that all the squabbles between the press and the management were irrelevant for the moment. All the moans about the amount of training seemed meaningless. The real message was that this was a team seriously in the mood to win the Test series.

The very act of committing such a thought to paper should have set all sorts of alarm bells ringing. To feel too good in the land of the world champions was to fall into a trap. And within days the Lions would be squirming in a pit. We should have seen it coming. Immediately after the game at Ballymore, Austin left the ground. This was not a good sign. 'Sorry,' he said, when I rang him on his mobile, 'but a couple of us just wanted to clear off.' He said he hadn't minded not going on from the replacements' bench because he'd been promised a start in the next game against Australia A the following Tuesday, but he sounded down.

'Anything else?' I asked.

'Usual crap,' he said. 'Popcorn. Casino.' I thought we had probably done popcorn and casino by now. This was a sticky moment. I had 750 words of Austin to produce for the paper and needed to be writing it now. As in: right now, Austin.

'Not much else,' he said. 'Oh yes,' he finally added, 'I thought Queensland were pretty rough, actually. We're here to play rugby and they just wanted to get stuck into us. There were a lot of incidents off the ball early on. That Toutai Kefu took Rob Howley out big time. We've got a problem with the local referees and can't wait for the neutrals to come in for the Tests. I thought the lads reacted really well. They stuck together and took no shit.'

Thank you, Austin. A spot of ref-bashing and accusations of foul play were perfect. And I was pretty convinced that he was right. With my own two eyes I had seen some of the incidents. The punch by Michael Foley on Rob Howley, for example. Somebody else was saying he had seen second row Mark Connors give Howley a dig, too. Come to think of it, the Welsh scrum half had had a bit of a night of it.

I bumped into him as we were leaving. He was walking gingerly down the stairs holding his ribs. 'That was pleasant, wasn't it?' he said wanly. 'Just what I needed.'

The Australians had a different version of the game. Even as the stories of Queensland excess were on their way to London, counter-accusations against the Lions were coming thick and fast. Their mouthpiece was Eddie Jones, coach of the Super 12 champions the ACT Brumbies, and of the Lions' next opponents, Australia A. He was also heir apparent to Rod Macqueen, the coach of the Wallabies who would be standing down in October.

Now that the Queensland game had failed to live up to its billing as the 'fourth Test', Australia A had become Test 4(a). And their coach was prepared to crank up the tension. He suggested that the Lions were responsible for all the incidents and that the next referee should keep a close eye on them, especially off the ball. The wars of 1989, when the Lions, according to Australian eyes – well, all eyes, really – resorted to intimidation and brutal means resurfaced. As we had all known at some stage they would.

Donal Lenihan did his best to defuse the situation. The Lions management had looked at the video of the Queensland game, he said, and found nothing untoward as far as their own players were concerned. And as for 1989, did not everybody realise that in twelve years rugby had completely changed and that there was little or no connection between the sport then and now?

Donal said this at a press conference at which on his left-hand side sat David Young. The Welsh prop was captain of the Tuesday team. He had also been a member of the 1989 Test side. He was, indeed, in the unique position of having gone on Lions tours across three decades: to Australia in 1989, South Africa in 1997 and back here to Australia in 2001. In fact, there was even more to the uniqueness of the David Young story. In 1987 he had been a teenager, combining a spot of playing in Canberra and seeing the world with his Swansea team-mate and fellow nineteen-year-old, Richard Webster, at the time of the first World Cup. Out of the blue they received a telephone call from the Welsh selectors and before they knew it they were both in Brisbane, making their Test debuts in a winning World Cup quarter-final against England. And if all that wasn't enough to cram into one career, David had also found time to have a spell in rugby league. He had been in the game a long time, had Dai. And old-hand front-row forwards tend to have a more fundamental view of the ways of rugby. I couldn't help but notice that he smiled slightly at Donal's comments about the changes in the game.

Donal nevertheless asked everyone to close the door once and for all on 1989. I saw Alex Spink afterwards and asked him if he was going to take that request to heart. Alex was the rugby correspondent on the *Mirror*. 'Absolutely not,' he said. 'My mob love all that.' And there was no chance at all that the Australian press were going to let it drop. This was propaganda.

8

Sydney first-time round. Part 1 for Australia A

By now we had moved from Brisbane to Sydney. To Manly, to be accurate, where we were staying in the Manly Pacific Parkroyal Hotel, facing not the harbour but the ocean. The graceful curve of the Brisbane River had given way to an arc of surf and sand. Wetsuits bobbed up and down in the waves or eased themselves upright on their boards and rode the tubes day and night. It all had that raw Aussie feel to it.

Manly was a rugby league suburb. Sydney was the Mecca of league. The thirteen-a-side code was big in Queensland, too, but in Sydney it was king. League was blue-collar beautiful in Sydney. Union was for the rich kids. There was far more in the papers about the daily bits and bobs of the league clubs than about the Wallabies, more about the decider of the State of Origin series between New South Wales and Queensland in two weeks' time than about the imminent arrival of the Lions and their forthcoming game against Australia A up the road in Gosford. Having said that, rugby union enjoyed more space than it used to. Once it had been worthy of a few short paragraphs on Test day.

Rugby union had pottered along in Australian sporting history, while other oval-ball games received the full treatment of publicity and media coverage. These others grew in popularity. Union was kept alive in private schools mostly run by the Catholic Church. Just as the Holy Ghost Fathers did much to keep rugby alive in Ireland at one time, so the Brothers and the Marists kept union alive while league was sweeping Sydney and Australian Rules the state of Victoria and across into South Australia. Union in Australia would probably never have blossomed beyond this Catholic courtyard had it not been for the influence and the rivalry of the country's distant neighbour across the Tasman Sea, New Zealand. But it was precisely because of this one single dimension that rugby union was now potentially big business even in Australia. Its single most powerful property was its international appeal. Rugby union was a multinational.

It was at first a British military phenomenon. Rugby went away with the armies of the Empire. The soldiers played it and the people of the towns they garrisoned adopted it, if only because it gave them a chance to give the Brits a good hammering at something. That was why Limerick in Ireland remained a rugby stronghold, through enmity not alliance. That was why the Welsh embraced rugby and did not join the great schism of 1895 when the northern English clubs broke away to create rugby league. To break away would have meant the end of the annual opportunity to beat England.

From military roots came commercial expansion. British traders took the game to France, Canada, Argentina and Uruguay. The French then took it to Romania, Italy and Spain. Russia and Georgia played rugby. The United States played rugby. Japanese companies liked the ethos of teamwork and developed rugby through their factories' sports clubs. The Pacific islands of Fiji, Samoa and Tonga loved it for its combination of running and big hits, especially the big hits.

Australian Rules meanwhile never grew out of Australia, except for an annual outing against the champions of Gaelic Football in Ireland. Rugby league remained confined to Australia and New Zealand, and in France and England, to corners whose land mass amounted to about a third of the size of Papua New Guinea, who incidentally also played the game.

Union's poly-national nature made it attractive, especially after the second great revolution, exactly one hundred years after the first, when in 1995 the game turned professional. The vague passions that rugby inspired could be converted into calculated investment. Rupert Murdoch's empire put in the money that created the Tri Nations, the annual competition involving South Africa, New Zealand and Australia. He bank-rolled the professional game in Britain through BSkyB Television.

Even in Australia there was a crisis in rugby league. One of the most famous clubs, South Sydney, had been forced out of existence. They had been known as the Rabbitohs after the cry of the players who were forced to supplement their rugby income during the 1930s with a spot of street-trading in meat. Surviving the Depression on two types of game. South Sydney didn't survive the 1990s. It was like striking Wigan off the map. They were victims of the turf war between the Australian Rugby league and Superleague, a commercial conflict that had ended only with the formation of a new body, the NRL. League's peace was uneasy. Clubs had been forced to amalgamate or, like the Rabbitohs, to disappear altogether as the top division shrank. Those that survived the reformation could not be guaranteed prosperity. One of the new, amalgamated franchises, the North-ern Eagles, was flat broke, it was reported while we were in Sydney. There was talk in the city, which I had first heard during the Olympics, that in the wake of the bitter battles and financial losses that had gone with the establishment of the NRL in Australia and Superleague in Britain, Murdoch might opt out of league in the long term. There was more commercial mileage in the game that better reflected his multinational view of the world. Rugby union.

The flow of talent from union to league was being reversed in Britain. Scott Quinnell, David Young and Scott Gibbs had all once followed a well-worn path out of Wales and gone north. But they had come south again. News came in daily of fresh approaches to players raised and steeped in league: Iestyn Harris of Leeds, Kris Radlinski of Wigan. Jason Robinson had already converted and was right now a Lion. Even in Australia players were being recruited against the grain of history. Wendell Sailor

'Train …

… train …

… train'

'All hell was about to break loose'

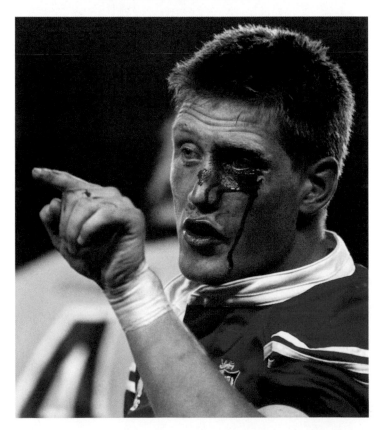

'The match went badly for the Lions ... This time there was an opposition that could make them pay'

The expression on the face of Robin McBryde says it all as the Lions crash to defeat against Australia A.

'Waltzing O'Driscoll'

Brian O'Driscoll on the break in the 1st Test.

'Jason was off, his dancing, darting running making you twitch in your seat'

Jason Robinson sidesteps around Stephen Larkham and Nathan Grey in the 1st Test.

Dafydd James scores the Lions' second try in the 1st Test.

'Scott Quinnell arrived, picked up and dived over … the contest was over'

Scott Quinnell is all smiles after powering through under the posts for the fourth Lions try in the 1st Test.

'The second half was one of the emotional highs of the tour'

Matt Dawson and Austin Healey celebrate the win over the ACT Brumbies.

'The atmosphere at the ground was echo-electric. A resonating pulse of sound went up and back down off the closed roof and then around the vast enclosure'

The 2nd Test at the Colonial Stadium, Melbourne.

'The Wallabies had rattled up a record team tally against the Lions ... the insurrectionists of Brisbane had been bushwacked in Melbourne'

John Eales celebrates winning the 2nd Test.

'Passers-by had to do a double-take to see if these really were the Lions players enjoying themselves'

Darren Morris in the surf on Manly Beach.

'If ever one name acted as a mood swingometer, it was Jonny's'

Jonny Wilkinson in the 3rd Test.

**'Kick ahead Ireland;
any feckin' head'**

Keith Wood kicks
ahead in the 3rd Test.

**'Keith Wood threw,
Johnson jumped …
and Justin Harrison
leapt across him and
won the ball'**

'Rod Macqueen could take his leave now, saying there was nothing left to win in the game'

Rod Macqueen congratulates Justin Harrison after the 3rd Test.

'For the Lions there was nothing, full-stop'

Rob Henderson, Keith Wood and Phil Vickery console each other in defeat.

and Mat Rogers were being lured out of league and into Super 12 franchises. Australian rugby union was no longer a sport kept alive by priests in private schools; the Wallabies were the world champions.

It was important to bear in mind, however, that the key phrase was 'in the long term'. Rugby league in Sydney was still king in 2001, and was already hitting back by saying it might target star Wallabies like George Gregan and Stephen Larkham in revenge raids. A press story appeared while we were in Sydney that the biggest catch in either code, Jonah Lomu of the New Zealand All Blacks, might be targeted by league.

League was fighting back on all fronts. Following a challenge in the appeal courts, news came amid wild celebrations at their old home at Redfern Oval that South Sydney were to be resurrected. The Rabbitohs were on their way back. The Northern Eagles said they might be having a little cash-flow difficulty, but the club was staying in business.

Rugby union still needed every juicy morsel to justify knocking league off the sports pages. The prospect of 'Filthy Lions Assaulting Our Boys – Again', was just the ticket. In private, Donal Lenihan no longer claimed this was an issue which had begun as some throwaway lines by Eddie Jones, or that the Australia A coach had been misquoted. The Lions manager had received correspondence from Jones on the headed notepaper of the Australian Rugby Union. The stakes were being raised.

The Lions announced their team to play Australia A in the fourth (a) Test. This was the last chance to make an impression before the real Test squad took shape. The team did not have the physical presence of the side that had outgunned Queensland. There was nothing exactly flimsy about the front row of Jason Leonard, Robin McBryde and Dai Young, but the second-row pairing were Scott Murray and Malcolm O'Kelly. Both were spring-heeled and lean; neither was a Martin Johnson. Graham Henry had said that some very fine second-row players were going to be very disappointed on this tour. Martin Johnson had the one spot that was set in stone, the number four shirt.

Captains did not lose their place on Lions tours. This left Scott Murray, Danny Grewcock, Jeremy Davidson and Malcolm O'Kelly competing for one middle-jumper position.

Danny Grewcock, expert in the martial arts, had to be the favourite. His typically abrasive performance against Queensland was complemented by some fine work on the opposition ball. When he was sent off on the Tour from Hell in 1998, against the All Blacks in Dunedin, it seemed incredible that someone so cherubic of mien could be guilty of the charges being levelled at him. Use of the boot? What, the man with the face of an angel? Three years later we knew that where Danny went, trouble tended to be his escort. He was excellent value in Australia.

Scott Murray and Danny Grewcock, until the latter's recent signing for Bath, had been team-mates at Saracens. Scott was a different type of animal, although he had tried to acquire Danny's taste for spicy rugby. In truth, he wasn't as . . . vigorous as his old mucker, excelling more in the pure arts. Like leaping with his basketball agility to win bonus ball on the opposition throw.

Malcolm O'Kelly was similarly athletic rather than heavy-weight, with a penchant for giving long miss-passes in the middle of the field. Jeremy Davidson played for Castres in France and would therefore know all about the nefarious side of lock play. But he had skills too. And experience of winning Lions tours. In fact he was the incumbent Lions number five, having forced his way into the Test team in South Africa. Danny Grewcock might be the favourite, but as the coach had said, some class acts were going to be left on the sideline.

The back row was going to be just as difficult to select. Richard Hill, Neil Back and Scott Quinnell had been shaping up nicely, when suddenly, out of nowhere, Martin Corry had added his name to the list of candidates. Colin Charvis and the Welsh open-side Martyn Williams had been conspicuous too, for that matter. And the options were hardly about to shrink. Lawrence Dallaglio was ready to take the field at last. His knee was fine, he said, and it was time to stake his claim.

In the three-quarters, Mike Catt was also about to make his first appearance of the tour. He had had first a bad back and then torn a calf muscle. This was his moment of reckoning, too. He had the familiar presence of Will Greenwood outside him, and no lack of experience inside him in the form of Neil Jenkins. On the wings were Jason Robinson and Ben Cohen, with Ben once again asked – sorry, told – to play on the right. Matt Perry was at fullback. There was possibly a place for sale here. Iain Balshaw had yet to reproduce the deadly stealth he had shown for England.

Austin was selected at scrum half. He was presented to the press conference, along with Martyn Williams and Lawrence Dallaglio. Austin sat and leaned over a piece of paper. He began to doodle. 'So, this is your last chance to make an impression,' came at him from the floor.

'Last and first,' came the reply. Austin went back to his doodling. 'You're losing your hair,' he scratched and showed to Lawrence Dallaglio.

Outside the press conference I passed Neil Jenkins. He was going to have his second outing of the tour. The outside half who held the record for most points in Test rugby – 1029 for Wales plus forty-one for the Lions in South Africa – had not been at his best in his first, in Townsville.

I wished him good luck. 'Has to be better than last week,' he said. 'Can't be any worse.' I said something about this being the moment to show them his true form. 'Ay, otherwise I may as well be on the plane home,' he said.

Neil had had to battle against all sorts of upsets in his rugby life. There was always someone a little faster, someone a little more creative in the position that carried folkloric responsibilities in Wales. Everyone wanted the Welsh outside half to be the next Cliff Morgan, David Watkins, Phil Bennett or Barry John; dancers, poets, weavers of spells. Neil was Neil, and he had battled against the lust for magic. In the new age there was no moondust, just eighteen-stoners bearing down on you. Besides, for what more magic could you ask than to win a Lions series with your kicking, as he had done in 1997? Or in 1999 kick the conversion to beat England 32–31 at Wembley in one of the most dramatic games of all time? Neil was Neil. But he didn't sound too full of self-belief at the moment. I didn't imagine the video camera I had brought him from Epsom racecourse had been out of its wrapper.

Somehow or other, Ian Robertson had managed to commandeer one of the Land Rovers supplied by the sponsors for the use of the team. It was never wise to ask how Robbo managed these things. The explanation was always as straightforward as the sub-paragraphs of the Common Agricultural Policy. Suffice it to say that he was very good at this wheeling and dealing, and we – Alastair Hignell, Robbo, their BBC producer Ed Marriage plus myself – set off for dinner. No doubt we were looking for one of the thousand restaurants where Robbo was a personal friend of the manager and where we would be rushed to the best table in the house. But, with Ed Marriage at the wheel, we found ourselves first heading the wrong way out of Manly and up a very steep hill towards Warringah. Then the Land Rover slipped into neutral between high and low ratio and suddenly we were going backwards towards Manly at rather an alarming speed.

Yes, the signs were there. We should have seen it coming. That night I woke at 4.30 a.m. and turned on the television. For a few sleepy moments I watched Michael Pechard on Australia Direct on BBC World. Australia had apparently ceased to be the dream eco-friendly wonder-world we imagined it to be. Great damage had been done. Pestilence was abroad. Surely, that was us, I thought groggily. Foot and mouth, and all that. But no. I drifted off to stories of purely Aussie plagues of rabbits, water hyacinths and fire ants clogging up every waterway, farm and garden of this vast land.

The next day I was minding my own business when three supporters approached. 'There's money on this,' said John, their leader. 'So, if I ask you a question you'd better be right.' They were a bit dusty for supporters, mind you. Real supporters kept their replica shirts spotless.

'That's right,' said their number two, Paul. 'A lot of money.'

'So, you'd better be right,' said Streaker, the third.

Streaker?

'Goes without saying,' said Paul.

Oh.

'If I'm not mistaken, lads,' I said, 'and I base this on the fact that I lived there for three years, I do believe you're from Gloucester.'

'Bristol, you daft old fool,' they all said.

'But now we live in Manly,' said Paul.

'Working on building sites,' said Streaker.

'I worked on the electrics at the Millennium Stadium,' said John. 'The roof and all that.'

Should I tell him that the roof and all that in Cardiff had broken down just before we came away? Probably not a good idea.

'Anyway,' said John, 'about this bet we've had . . .'

'A big one,' said Paul.

'How many Welshmen are going to get in the Test team?'

'Well, it's hard to say at the moment because a lot depends on the game tomorrow against . . .'

'Never mind all that,' said Paul. 'I said three.'

'Two,' said Streaker.

'And I said none,' said John. 'Bloody Welsh.'

'Could be four,' I said.

'Four?' they exploded. 'And who would they be?'

'Scott Quinnell, Rob Howley, Dafydd James and Darren Morris.'

'Who the fuck is Darren Morris?' they shouted. 'You'd better be wrong.' And they went dustily on their way.

A few days later I was having a jar with Donal Lenihan and he said that the coaches reckoned that if Darren, loosehead prop of Swansea and Wales, only believed in himself, he could be the world-class sensation of the tour. He was big and strong, ferocious in the tackle, but also light on his feet and armed with a delicate touch with the ball in his hands.

But first we had to get through the Tuesday-night game, the one stirred up by Eddie Jones, one for which Darren Morris was only sitting on the bench. It was to be played at another of those grounds named with romance in mind: the North Power Stadium in Gosford. It was a brand new stadium with a capacity of twenty-five thousand. It had stands on three sides, the eastern end having been left open to allow views from within of the adjacent marina.

Although it was a multi-purpose stadium, North Power was best known for being one of the homes of that rugby league club with cash-flow problems, the Northern Eagles, which was an amalgamation of three clubs: Manly, North Sydney and Gosford's Central Coast. The new club played half their home games at Brookvale Oval near our Manly hotel and half here in Gosford. Their clubhouse across the road from the main stand was gigantic. Our press party was setting records for being the biggest ever to travel with a rugby union side, but we were lost in the cavernous media area. And you could have fitted a dozen of those areas into the ballroom next door. And the ballroom was nothing compared to the bars downstairs. There were enough poker machines – pokies – to stretch from Gosford to Las Vegas, and a ten-dollar spread of food laid out for the punters that would have filled Lake Taho. In New South Wales rugby league was still king.

King with a dirty finger, however. Permit me for a moment to dive down this little side-track. Or this little back passage, really.

John Hopoate, originally from Tonga, had once been a player at the Northern Eagles, before going onward and upward to Wests. His career had rather publicly been put on hold because he was caught several times, at the tackle area, inserting his finger . . . er, um, up the rear-end of the player he was tackling. I suppose it was to encourage him to let go of the ball. Stripping, they call this stealing of the ball, although it doesn't usually involve quite such an act of penetration.

Hopoate had been banned and was now working his way back. Rehabilitating himself, I mean. Manly had offered him a contract in the lower grades, and if that went well, he might go back to Wests via Northern Eagles. And why was he being so readily pardoned for his sins of the posterior?

'Aw, come on, guys,' said Northern Eagles manager Wayne Beavis, 'he didn't shit in the Queen's handbag.'

The match went badly for the Lions. Everybody was too anxious again, too keen to impress again. This time there was an opposition that could make them pay. In the opening minutes Austin had to cover back to prevent a try. The impressive wing forward David Lyons burst through Mike Catt to set up a chance for another. The Lions held out, but they were fully stretched.

The line-out was not functioning. The reception and chasing of restarts were worse. The jumpers were outmuscled by Tom Bowman and Justin Harrison in the Australia A second row, and hooker Robin McBryde was having trouble finding his targets with his throws. He had spent so much time concentrating on recovering from the dead leg he had received in Townsville that he had just lost the knack of chucking the ball in. Neil Jenkins had another difficult game. He was simply a shadow of the calm, determined player he could be. He was often caught in two minds. He hit the post with his first shot at goal and then struck a second penalty attempt over, but the A open side Phil Waugh was on his case.

Austin at scrum half was trying too hard, like all the others. Even Lawrence Dallaglio was making mistakes, missing tackles he could make in his sleep when match-hardened. One such miss, on Nathan Grey, led to a penalty. Outside half Manny Edmonds kicked it, a second to add to a first awarded against Malcolm O'Kelly for offside. Australia A were in the lead.

The penalties kept coming their way. A pass infield by Will Greenwood led only to trouble for the Lions deep in their own half. The ball was turned over, the Lions infringed and Edmonds kicked penalty number three. The Lions were then offside. Number four. Offside again. Five.

And between those fourth and fifth penalties the picture grew even gloomier for the Lions. Chasing a kick downfield, Mike Catt pulled up lame. His calf muscle had gone again. Mark Taylor came on as a replacement. At half-time the Lions, for the first time on tour, were trailing. 6–15.

They began the second half in positive vein. They kicked penalties not at goal but to the corners and went for the try. But a bad line-out led to a break-out by Australia A and only the covering Ben Cohen prevented a try at the other end of the field. The Lions rang the changes to save the line-out. Jeremy Davidson and Gordon Bulloch came on for Malcolm O'Kelly and Robin McBryde. It made no immediate difference. First, there was a scrum to survive. From it the A team moved the ball down the backline, unwittingly foxing the Lions with a pass into midfield that bounced along the floor. Centre Graeme Bond – ex league, fine player – cut inside Ben Cohen for winger Scott Staniforth to score. A try from set-piece. Phil Larder would be going ape.

More changes. Sam Payne came on for scrum half Chris Whitaker. This at least offered some relief for the Lions. Whitaker had been outstanding. Matt Dawson came on for the unhappy Neil Jenkins. Or rather he came on at scrum half and Austin moved to outside half.

The Lions scrambled their way back into the game. The new scrum half took a penalty quickly and sent Mark Taylor over for the try.

Patricio Noriega, the Puma prop from Perth, appeared off the bench just in time to watch at close-hand Manny Edmonds kick his sixth penalty. The Lions trailed by a nasty margin, twelve points.

More changes. This was a rush-hour of replacements: Jono West for Tom Bowman, Darren Morris for Dai Young, Peter Ryan for Jim Williams, the number eight courted by Declan Kidney of Munster. The Lions missed a chance when a slightly fancy flip behind his back by Will Greenwood hit the deck and bounced away.

Then, more trouble. Lawrence Dallaglio dipped his hands

once too often into the ruck and was sent to the sin-bin. The Lions were down to fourteen players. And down by fifteen points as penalty number seven went over.

The A team brought on more fresh legs to try to make the advantage tell: Tom Murphy for Brendan Cannon at hooker. So many names, but worth remembering. This was the next generation, coached by the next coach of the Wallabies, Eddie Jones. And they were all doing a fine job.

The Lions nearly mugged them. Unbelievable. They were in such desperate trouble and they nearly pinched the game. Or at least they nearly snatched a draw. Matt Dawson missed a simple penalty. It hardly mattered, we thought. The game was up. But then – and while still down to fourteen – Mark Taylor made a break for Matt Perry to cross. Two minutes later, Dawson combined with all sorts, including Will Greenwood, Martyn Williams, Jeremy Davidson and finally Jason Robinson. Dawson converted both tries. 25–28. Game over. Game lost. Close but lost.

This was no time to go on the defensive and look for excuses. But . . . but even the Lions in this ropy form were better than the referee. This was the first time they had been given a neutral arbiter for a game, but if Paul Honiss of New Zealand was anything to go by, they stood a better chance with a home Australian in charge.

Honiss had last been seen in Rome, officiating in the Italy – Wales game in the Six Nations. He had messed up that game, too. The Roman night for the media corps had been dedicated to slagging off this overzealous whistle-blower. For some reason, at two o'clock in the morning I had bumped into him at the official function. Committeemen and their wives were bopping the night away, which was fine as long as you were Italian and could do cool at any hour of the day or night.

It was another 'Donal' moment, like the 'nip in the bud' night in Townsville. As Rome slept all around us I had allowed this referee to tell me all about how disappointed he was that neither Italy nor Wales had done what he ordered them to do. I did not say that he, not they, had ruined the game.

And here he was again, blasting away by whistle and mouth, completely out of touch with the spirit of the night. No doubt, he received top marks from his assessor for technical merit. But he was a shocker.

The Lions had lost. Their win-all-on-tour bonus of something like five thousand pounds a man, it was suggested, was down the drain. Donal Lenihan gave them a tongue-lashing in the changing room, not so much on the financial grounds but on the matter of letting down the shirt.

It was perhaps a touch harsh. The midweek teams from the outset had had little time to prepare. Sunday was generally a travel day, which left them Monday to plan their moves. And even then, the Saturday side had begun to ask them to come over and pretend to be Australia. The dirt-trackers had every right to feel slightly neglected.

On the other hand, Australia A had been a side well drilled by Eddie Jones. The coach also appeared to have won the mental sparring. After his comments about the rough-house Lions, he said the game in the end had been played in a good spirit. Although they would be looking at the video to see if the tackle by Ben Cohen, which had fractured the cheekbone of fullback Richard Graham, was dangerous and worthy of a citing. It was one last barb by the Australian camp on the night. The Lions had to take it, turn around and head back down the road to Manly.

9

Still in Sydney: Part 1(b)

There was to be no let-up on the propaganda front. Eddie Jones departed with that final aside concerning an incident about which nothing more was heard, and Bob Dwyer took his place. Bob had a wonderful track-record in the game, having been coach of the Wallabies when they won the World Cup in 1991. He had coached New South Wales at state level and Randwick, the most successful of the Sydney clubs, at the time when the Ella brothers, Mark, Gary and Glen, were reinventing the way the ball could be moved down a flat backline of three-quarters. He had coached in Europe, with Stade Français briefly in Paris, and with Leicester and Bristol in England. And everywhere he had been, he was colourful and controversial.

His time in England had been quite as glitteringly successful as the first part of his career in Australia. With Leicester he had attempted to remould the ways of the most fiercely protective rugby family in the land, and had been shunned and squeezed out by the senior players, including Martin Johnson. Bob had not lasted long at Bristol, either. So, here he was, back in Australia as coach of the New South Wales Waratahs, the Lions' next opponents. Just by way of variety, he was also a guest columnist for our *Sunday Times*. And since he was always available for a comment or two in his local *Sydney Morning Herald* or *Telegraph* it is fair to say that there was no shortage of space for Bob Dwyer to have his say on the Lions. He went for a few compliments, saying how formidable the tourists could be, how stacked with class players they were, and he went for a spot of colour. He said that the Lions cheated at the scrum, the line-out and the breakdown. It was the same as before, with the name of B. Dwyer instead of E. Jones as the source, but it helped fuel the build-up, which was exactly the aim: to sell the game by promoting the Lions as the bad guys.

Meanwhile our press corps was wading in as well. Into the swell of the Tasman Sea, that is. Adidas, one of the tour suppliers and sponsors, had organised an afternoon of beach activities for the media and the players. We all turned up; the Lions did not. Adidas didn't put out a press release on how much it cost them for the hire of the Freshwater Surf Lifesaving Club, for the spread of food, the beach-volleyball referees and the surfing instructors, but they couldn't have been overwhelmed by the absence of the star turns. Instead, they had to entertain . . . us. We did our best to behave like international superstars, but if I were still out there now on the ocean wave, there is no way I could ever lift my frame, crammed as it was into a wetsuit designed for a size-six supermodel, into an upright position on that ironing board. We did our bit, then, coughing and spluttering or nursing sand-burns from the volleyball, made our excuses about deadlines, deadlines, and limped away.

   That night we recovered by indulging in something far dearer to our cultural proclivities. We went to the opera. No, not the opera, but the Sydney Opera. We took the catamaran – on a free-fare day, thanks to ongoing industrial action – for one of the most majestic harbour-crossings in the world, from Manly to Sydney. We strolled from Circular Quay to one of the great architectural masterpieces of the world. We downed several glasses of bubbly by moonlight on a balcony facing the Bridge and then we took our seats in the very back row of the highest gods for our dose of Puccini. *Il Trittico*, which Giacomo knocked off in 1917.

   If you ask me, the middle bit of the first of the triptych, *Il Tabarro*, was a bit ponderous. During the first interval, six of the eight of us in our row confessed to nodding off. In the second, *Suor Angelica*, I dropped off again.

More bubbly. And then back for the third and last of the triptych, *Gianni Schicchi*. This was more like it. We all sang along to '*O mio babbino caro*', which must have been used in an advert for BMW or something. We said that Simone the eldest of the Donatis, looked just like Jack Rowell, the former England coach, we shouted 'Bravissimo', a few times and made our exit in time for the last cat back across the bay.

I ran into Donal Lenihan in the hotel lobby. We went for a jar. He'd already had a few, had Donal, and was all cuddly about his players. He said they had responded to the crisis of Tuesday evening brilliantly. The midweek team had made a special effort to go over and support the Saturday team as it prepared to take on Bob Dwyer's Waratahs. I asked him about the back row. Richard Hill had not been selected. Neil Back, Lawrence Dallaglio and Scott Quinnell were the chosen combination. Were they seriously considering leaving out Hill for the tests? He said Hill, off the record, was a dead cert. This was even sweeter music to my ears than Puccini, for I had told the paper that I wanted to do a feature on the Saracens and England wing forward, and had put in a request to see him the next day.

Austin came into the bar. Tomorrow was a day off for the players. He'd been out. He'd had a few more than Donal and was at his most pesky. He'd been to this seafood restaurant that everybody had been talking about, Doyle's on Circular Quay, with some of the lads. Just like Grimsby Fisheries on Welford Road in Leicester, Austin reckoned. Now he was going to finish off his evening by winding everyone up. He asked me if the *Guardian* was a right-wing newspaper. I left him as he was telling Donal how he thought you should only be allowed to play for the country in which you were born. People had to make sacrifices, Donal; even mothers in labour.

The next day turned into a chase for players. The original plan had been to see Austin first thing for Friday's *Guardian*, but given his slight squiffiness of the night before, I had told him we could meet up later.

As a preview to the first Test at the Gabba in Brisbane, the *Observer* wanted me to profile a player from each side. I phoned up Djuro Sen, media manager of the Wallabies at the Pacific Bay Resort way up the coast of New South Wales in Coffs Harbour. I put in a request for George Gregan, the scrum half the Lions would have to stop. Djuro said he would phone back in an hour. Yeah, sure, I thought.

Sixty minutes later Djuro rang and handed the phone to George himself. And very obliging George was, too, without of course giving away anything remotely resembling a juicy titbit from the Wallabies' camp. He was on a roll, having captained the ACT Brumbies to victory in the Super 12. This was doubly special because George, unlike many of the Brumbies who had been shipped in from other states to beef up the ACT squad when it first gained its Super 12 franchise, had been brought up in Canberra. Local boy makes good.

Not quite. George had been schooled at St Edmund's College in Canberra but he had been born in Zambia, like Dafydd James, the Lions wing. According to Austin, this should have precluded them from representing Australia and Wales respectively. Think of the side Zambia might have by now.

I went down to the foyer to meet Austin. He had said he was on his way back from the golf course and would be there at two o'clock. I wasn't to tell anyone he'd been playing golf because injured players weren't supposed to do anything but rest.

I came down in the lift as he was going up the stairs to the first floor, to the exclusive province of the players. Damn. Having joined in the general groan about the lack of punctuality among the Lions, I'd now missed my man.

A few minutes later, however, Alex Broun came down and showed me up into the players' room. The inner sanctum. Austin was lying on the physio bench while Mark Davies packed ice on his backside. Mark had been a contemporary of mine on the field. He used to play for Swansea in the back row and was capped three times by Wales. He had been on that B tour to Spain in 1983. Mark was a strong, silent type. He had had a six-pack stomach long before they became a fashion item. He had the same nickname now as he had had then: 'Carcass'.

Quietly Mark packed the ice on Austin's rear. 'A bruised buttock,' said Austin. 'A dead arse.' Somebody had kneed him there during the A game. It wasn't the only time he had been in danger. At one stage he was hauled out of a ruck by the giant ACT second row, Justin Harrison, and manhandled towards the touchline. Austin had spread his arms out and looked up at the player towering over him.

What had happened to provoke all this? 'Will Greenwood was having a right old shoeing at the ruck,' said Austin. 'This one bloke kicked him twice in the head. So, I upper-cutted him. Can't have that. The trouble was that Harrison saw me do it. So, he started to chase me. I tell you what: he was lucky I was in a good mood. I was about to throw him into the stand.'

Even the quiet Carcass paused. 'No,' admitted Austin, 'what really happened was that this giant had hold of me and I held out my arms and said, "Go on then, hit me." If he had, he'd have been sent off.'

Austin had not played that well. He was the only player who had been selected in the squad of twenty-two for all four games, but this had been his first time in the starting line-up. He had been trying too hard. And the ball from the forwards had been slow or non-existent in the first half. In the second he had gone to outside half and things had improved, but he was not in contention for a Test slot at number ten.

Carcass was by now removing the ice and starting to examine a large red and blue bruise.

'I suppose when things go wrong,' continued Austin, 'they blame the decision-makers. And I'm one of them.'

I left him shouting in pain as Carcass dug a strong, silent physio's finger into the bruise of a dead arse.

One more to go in my triptych of players. Richard Hill. He arrived on time and we went out onto the first-floor balcony. He was a strong, silent type, too, although he began by talking about koi carp that had been sucked up by a mini tornado out of a pond in Salisbury, where he had been brought up, and dumped on the South Wilts golf course. He then settled into tour-talk. It was difficult to ignore the banter about over-training and boredom emanating from the camp. Players were starting to resent the sheer slog of it all. Austin had told me.

But not Richard Hill. He said it had to be done. This was their job. This was what you had to do if you wanted to beat the world champions. And if it so happened that, contrary to a little whisper I had heard, he was not selected for the first Test, then no, he would not sulk or be angry or tell the world how hard-done-by he was. He would expect, but not demand, an explanation from the coaches, and then he would do his best to help the chosen squad achieve that single goal of beating Australia.

Richard Hill was a fantastic player. He was a genius at doing two hundred things to perfection and yet giving the impression of having a quiet game. He was one of those players whose contribution could only be appreciated by reviewing games on videotape. How did he manage to get from there to there, from making a try-saving tackle to giving an unseen, slipped pass that turned a whole movement around? If things were ever so bad in an alley-fight that you needed more help even than Martin Johnson, Richard Hill would do. Nobody would know how all those assailants were suddenly lying in a neat pile. He would make a very good spy.

The Friday morning papers of Sydney contained more inflammatory stuff about the game ahead. At the Thursday afternoon press conference Andy Robinson had made some entirely measured remarks about the Lions' approach to the scrummage. The Lions wanted to scrum hard; they wanted to be allowed to do so by referees who seemed keener to award free kicks and penalties at the primary set-piece. On Friday morning these comments were presented as the Lions snarling back in the war of words.

We had only sad news to report. Mike Catt's tour was over. His calf had gone again, and that was that. Word then reached us that Dan Luger had had a 'freak accident' in training, a clash of heads with Neil Back, and was doubtful. Doubtful for what? Saturday's game? The rest of the tour? The x-rays would tell.

They revealed a fracture to his cheek, just below the eye. Luger was out of the tour. The winger, who had been a certainty to play in the Tests, had broken down again. Poor Luger had had a season wrecked by one injury after another. He had battled to be fit in time to tour and now, even as his parents were winging in to watch him, he was leaving.

The Lions had not selected Richard Hill on the blind side for the game against the Waratahs, preferring to give Lawrence Dallaglio another chance to prove his fitness. Nor had they considered Rob Howley, who was nursing rib-cartilage damage. Matt Dawson came in at scrum half. Apart from the two RH's, Richard Hill and Robert Howley, and the now absent Luger and Catt, it looked very much a Test side.

Will Greenwood was partnering Brian O'Driscoll in the centre. Jason Robinson on the left and Dafydd James on the right were the wingers. Iain Balshaw, perhaps the player under most pressure to hit peak form, was selected at fullback.

The pack had a Celtic fringe to it. The book-ends of the forwards were Darren Morris and Keith Wood at one and two, and Scott Quinnell at eight. The five places in between were all English: Phil Vickery, Martin Johnson, Danny Grewcock, Lawrence Dallaglio and Neil Back. As a sandwich filling it was gruesome, and just what was required if the Lions were to bounce back from their midweek upset.

We, the press, decided to share the discomforts and pain of serious competition. Paul Morgan booked the rugby ground just behind the hotel and we trooped down to Manly Oval for a game of football. Soccer, rather, as the ground-staff called it, as they made way for this effete bunch of failed surfers. We – my side – won 4–3, by the way, thanks to the workrate of Andy Howell of the *Western Mail* on the left wing, and an influx of Scottish midfielders in the third quarter. Don't ask.

I went for a swim afterwards, worn out by playing in goal. I nearly rammed an elderly resident of the parish who was drifting in front of me. 'Steady dear,' she said, 'I'm eighty-one years old.

My bones are busted and my muscles wasted. My doctor tells me
to swim every day, so I do. I'm like a jellyfish out here.' She told
me her name but a wave hit me. I think it was Alice. Or was it
Grace? Anyway, she bobbed up gracefully with the wave while I
had my ears filled with water.

Alice/Grace's father had grown potatoes as a tenant farmer
near Stonehenge. He'd come to Australia and had become a
train-driver in the Valley of Lithgow on the way through the
Blue Mountains. He'd gone back to Europe to drive trains in
France in the First World War and had returned to Australia
stone-deaf. He never talked about it. Alice/Grace had been a
secretary and had hated it. Now she loved lying in the water like
a jellyfish in her little corner of paradise. She told me to save
plenty of money for the bad times and floated away on another
wave.

On Saturday the war of words became the war-game. The Lions
against the Waratahs. The match was played at Sydney Football
Stadium, which lay right next door to the Sydney Cricket
Ground. It was a sell-out of forty thousand, the largest crowd
ever to watch a non-Test game of rugby in Australia.

It took all of three seconds for referee Scott Young from
Queensland to send his first player of the night to the sin-bin.
Touch judge Stu Dickinson, who had refereed the Lions against
Queensland at Ballymore, saw Waratah second row Tom Bow-
man aim a forearm smash at Danny Grewcock at the kick-off.
He told the referee and Bowman was off for ten minutes before
he had even had a chance to draw breath, let alone run out of it.

The clear warning by the referee did not stop the process of
fermentation. Neil Back had his head stamped on in the first half.
Punches were half-thrown. Something was brewing. While that
was going on as a sub-theme, the Lions were playing well. Up front
they were solid against a pack that contained five of the A
forwards who had embarrassed the midweek team in Gosford.
The Lions scored a try after just three minutes. Danny Grewcock
won a line-out, Brian O'Driscoll went on one run, and then
another after a burst by Scott Quinnell. Neil Back was the link

to Jason Robinson before O'Driscoll became involved for the third time, this time as the try-scorer. If the Irish centre had waited until the second half to declare himself to Brisbane, he was showing Sydney how good he was from the very off. His understanding with Jonny Wilkinson was special. Neil Back was everywhere, locked in a personal duel on the open side with the Waratahs' captain Phil Waugh. Waugh was a player very much in the mould of George Smith, the back-row sensation of the full Wallabies team. It was necessary to tie him up early in the chain of phase-plays. Scott Quinnell was picking up the ball, driving low and then twisting out of the tackle to make extra yards.

And Jason Robinson was playing so well on the left wing that the loss of Dan Luger was already not hurting so much. Robinson seemed to be saying, 'Remember those things you said I couldn't do in Perth, like turn to present the ball in the tackle? Well, watch this. Is that good enough?' It was. 'Is this OK?' as he ran in his seventh try of the tour. 'And this?' as he supported Iain Balshaw under a high ball and then leapt on his own to claim another. 'You think I can't tackle?' as he drove a Waratah five metres into touch. By the time he ran in for his eighth tour try, standing in at scrum half for Matt Dawson, who was buried, and bursting through a mesmerised defence, his case was made. Nobody was finding fault tonight.

Not everybody was in sublime nick. There was still the riddle of Iain Balshaw to solve. Not long after Brian O'Driscoll's opening try the fullback caught a ball in his own twenty-two and thought about launching a counterattack. He hesitated and then decided to go for it. But the hesitation was costly. He was collared and robbed of the ball. The Waratahs scored through wing forward Stu Pinkerton.

It had always been known that there would be injuries on tour. That players would lose form. But Iain Balshaw was such an ace in the Lions' hand. And the worst thing was that if things were going wrong for a running fullback, they were going wrong in full view of everyone. Forty thousand spectators were watching the blond, coltish sensation of Twickenham being reduced to a nervous wreck in Oz.

Others were also in agony. Lawrence Dallaglio went down clutching his bad knee. That was that . . . but no, he carried on. Then Will Greenwood stayed down after a tackle. He couldn't carry on and limped off on a badly twisted ankle. Ronan O'Gara took to the field in his place.

The Lions still led handsomely at half-time, 24–5. But pain inflicted legitimately, whether on the mind of Iain Balshaw or the ankle of Will Greenwood, was about to grow more acute. The infection started fairly enough. The Waratahs, nineteen points adrift, scored twice through wing Francis Cullimore and centre Sam Harris, running through a defence that, without Greenwood, wasn't quite as solid as it had been in the first period. This was intriguing. Questions were being asked in a contest that had seemed as good as settled. The gap was now seven points.

All hell was about to break loose. A movement broke down not far from the Waratahs' line. An attack by the Lions had petered out. Suddenly all eyes turned to the small figure of Duncan McRae, the Waratahs' fullback, who had the even smaller Ronan O'Gara pinned down and was repeatedly punching him. As the victim would say later, he was trying to make amends for losing a couple of balls earlier. He had cleaned out a ruck – that is, after a tackle he had driven in and over the ball, taking out McRae by legitimate means – and found himself held. The fullback had taken offence at something. He would later claim he was struck by a kick, then a swinging arm. He punched O'Gara time and again. Eleven times, the replays would suggest. O'Gara left the field with blood streaming from a cut below his eye. He was shaking his head and waving an arm in disgust. Was this McRae's revenge by proxy on Martin Johnson for breaking his ribs while he was at Saracens?

Scott Young sent McRae off. Could we please return to the rugby? Having sent off the Waratahs' fullback, the referee had barely restarted the game when he was sending more players from the field. A mass brawl broke out and two from each side were sent to the sin-bin: Danny Grewcock and Phil Vickery from the Lions, hooker Brendan Cannon and prop Cameron Blades from the Waratahs.

Because two front-row forwards had been lost, the Waratahs began to put on replacements for any scrummages. Players wandered on and off at will. If the comings and goings had been frequent in Gosford, this was now bafflingly complicated. The game was reduced to farce. For the record, Jonny Wilkinson and Dafydd James scored tries to seal victory for the Lions, while Manny Edmonds scored a late try for the home side.

The press conference afterwards was lively. Donal Lenihan condemned McRae's act and said he hoped the Waratahs would not be able to manage their way out of this one. He added that the Australians were very good at such management.

Bob Dwyer said that McRae was sorry. He said nobody defended the action. It was bad for the game. And then he tried to manage the damage. Look, the Waratahs had been angelic in the Super 12. They weren't brawlers. And if they had gone looking for trouble here they would hardly have looked to little McRae to lead the charge. Furthermore, the first punch of the night had been thrown not by a Waratah but by Danny Grewcock, after thirty seconds. And the first punch to be thrown and penalised had been by Phil Vickery after one minute. So, it wasn't all one-way traffic.

Austin came in and stood at the back of the press conference. He pointed to his mouth and to his backside. Bob was talking out of it. Austin was not surprised by the violence, since he was pretty sure there was a conspiracy afoot to soften up the tourists by just about any means. He was convinced a propaganda war was raging. He said it was hard enough trying to have any fun on tour in the first place, given the regime, but when the Aussies started coming at you from all angles it made life even tougher. The changing room was a mess after the game but the Lions were more determined than ever to win out here.

I tried to put it to Bob that, given the generation of ill-feeling in the build-up to this game – a process in which he had played no small part – the explosion on the field had been almost inevitable.

He said I had played for a dirty team. And no, he didn't feel responsible. Well, that was that then.

All the banter leading up to this had turned sour. But if it was portrayed as an intercontinental antagonism, its roots lay in a couple of backyard tiffs. Most of the antagonistic comments had come from Bob Dwyer, who must have believed his contempt was well founded. He had suffered a rare failure as a coach in England. How much respect did he have for the game there?

Duncan McRae, too, had a personal axe to grind. He had not been considered indispensable to Saracens. What was more galling was his hospitalisation by the captain of Leicester and the Lions. He could hardly have launched a solo mission of revenge as a replacement in the company of strangers in Perth. But in Sydney he was on home soil. Where better to exact retribution for what had happened to him in Britain? Except, of course, that he picked on an Irishman.

Improved global communications, agents and managers had transformed rugby. The British and Irish game was awash with players and coaches from other rugby cultures. Little came as a surprise in the game now. Curiosity about players from the other side of the world had been replaced by a familiarity through regular contact. There were no secrets. The sense of facing the unknown and being apprehensive about what an opponent might offer was replaced by knowledge of what he could not deliver. There was a lack of respect between people who knew each other well.

The irony was that these personal enmities through frequent contact were erupting around a game with the Lions, who only visited once every twelve years. Dormant bitterness from 1989 and live frustrations appeared to be a volatile mix. The brawls of the New South Wales encounter were hardly on a par with the Lions' game against Canterbury in 1971. This had been a savage running battle, at the end of which Sandy Carmichael of Scotland had a face that made Ronan O'Gara look as unblemished as an air-brushed Pear's baby. But in the context of what was tolerable in the professional age it was way over the mark.

Ronan O'Gara, with a left eye so swollen that it could not

open, was summoned to McRae's disciplinary meeting at 9.30 the following morning. Nothing was found on videotape to implicate the Irishman in any act of foul play. McRae was handed down a seven-week ban.

10

Up the coast to Coffs Harbour

Ronan O'Gara wasn't the only player out of the hotel early on the Sunday morning. Before nine o'clock, Will Greenwood was carefully placed in the back of a Land Rover and was driven by James Robson, the team doctor, north towards Gosford for an MRI scan on his ankle. They would then keep heading up the coast of New South Wales to Coffs Harbour, the resort where the Wallabies had made their camp and where the Lions would play their last game before the Brisbane Test. Australia, the size of Jupiter, now had the two Test teams lodging within a couple of miles of each other.

That was the transport arrangement for a crocked centre. We were going by air. Only small planes flew into Coffs Harbour, so our party was divided into three groups for flights in the early and late morning and the early afternoon. I was on the middle flight. As a handful of us were waiting to catch a bus to take us out to the fifty-seater propeller plane on the tarmac, the flight attendant asked us where we were all from. She was given the names of a few strange corners of home, before a woman who was not a member of our party said, 'I am from Russia. My God, I hope this plane is not going to crash.'

She laughed. Nervously. We all boarded the aircraft, which taxied out to the runway, revved furiously, began to roll and then stopped.

'Sorry, ladies and gentlemen,' said the pilot. 'We seem to have a light showing here. We're going to taxi to a quiet spot, test the engines again and see if we can't be on our way.'

The engines revved again. 'No, sorry, we've still got a light on here.' We taxied back to the terminal. White smoke was coming out of the back of the left engine. As we disembarked, an engineer appeared holding two cans of aviation oil and a screwdriver. Somehow, I thought it might be more electro-technical than that. 'Don't worry,' said the attendant, 'they're putting you on a different plane.'

Soon we were on board a plane that had been due to go to Dubbo. 'Don't worry, now,' said the Russian passenger. 'This is a good plane. I feel these things.'

'Welcome to Coffs Harbour,' said the sign at the airport where we landed safely. 'Home of the Wallabies. The World Champions, the Tri Nations Champions and holders of the Bledisloe Cup.' The town had done a deal with the Wallabies, and the Pacific Bay Resort was their base for Test preparation. The Lions were staying up the road in another hotel resort, the Novotel Opal Cove. We were with the Wallabies.

The very first person I saw at the Pacific Bay was John Eales. He came wandering into reception with a bag of laundry between his teeth and a child on either arm. The captain of the world champions greeted us and asked what we thought of the Lions game in Sydney. We mumbled something inoffensive. What did he think of it? 'Yeah, it was kind of weird, wasn't it?' John Eales was such an all-round good egg that it was difficult to link him with any conspiracy, especially when he was bouncing a one-year-old on his knee. Rod Macqueen, coach of the Wallabies walked by and welcomed us. What did we think of the game? Mumble, mumble. What did he think of it? 'It came as a bit of a shock,' he said. He had been quoted as saying that in the Tests, 'sanity would surely prevail'. The Wallaby camp was spreading out a fire blanket.

The hotel rooms were more like apartments, placed in units all over the complex. There were tennis courts and swimming pools and a nine-hole par-three golf course, everything a hundred yards from the beach. It was easy to be hyper-critical on these ventures, but this was all a bit . . . contrived. And when the pneumatic drills started up at seven in the morning on the site of the Marine Science Centre, under construction mere feet from our apartment blocks, it was all too tempting to sew back together the strands of the Australian plot to derail the Lions and all who travelled with them.

On the evening of our arrival in this strange, sprawling town on the New South Wales coastline we were all sitting around in the bar when Alex Broun appeared. This was unusual. Normally we had to travel to the Lions. Here was their messenger bringing us news. It had to be bad.

James Robson, who had been on the road all day, had arrived in Coffs Harbour and had only now finished assessing players, other than Will Greenwood, damaged the night before. The news was that . . . we all supposed he was going to say that the scan had confirmed that Greenwood's tour was over. But no, as far as the centre was concerned, he would not be available for the first Test but would be reassessed in a couple of days, when the swelling around his ankle went down. The medical team were reasonably certain that he would be available for selection for the second and third Tests. Then came the bad news. Lawrence Dallaglio would not be playing in any of the Tests. The bang to his knee had aggravated the old injury and he would be going home the following Sunday. David Wallace of Munster, the youngest of the Test-playing Wallace brothers, after wing Richard and prop Paul, had been sent for as a replacement. I remembered doing a piece for television on Richard who, as a hobby, flew light aircraft. We took off from a runway somewhere near Shannon, but only after Richard had rummaged around in his pockets muttering, 'Now, where did I put the keys?' We circled a few times over the ribbon of the River Shannon and the lush landscape around Limerick and then prepared to land. 'This is not my strong point,' said Richard. 'And that,' and here he pointed to what looked like a black matchstick on the green expanses, 'is the shortest runway in Ireland.'

Without wishing to give the impression that an infallible theory had been disproved, I felt that my analysis of ligament damage, the one which went back nearly two decades to my time of Cup Final disappointment followed by an almost immediate tightening of the knee joint, had been undermined. Those wretched fibres were meant to have regained their strength by now. Lawrence must have suspected all the while that he was too wobbly of joint to survive the tour. To opt to play in the knowledge that you are likely to go down with a searing, possibly crippling, pain is a rare decision to have to take.

That wasn't the end of the medical bulletin. Keith Wood had an unspecified leg problem and Robin McBryde had a new bruise on his dead leg. The Lions needed cover at hooker. Dorian West of Leicester and England had been summoned.

Two new players were on their way. Two more had just arrived. Scott Gibbs for Mike Catt, and Tyrone Howe for Dan Luger. The Welsh centre was on his third Lions tour, having been to New Zealand in 1993 and South Africa – where he had been player of the series – in 1997. Tyrone, of Ulster, was on his first tour. Coffs Harbour was no longer a resort of dubious charm but a field hospital. However natural it seemed to see Scott Gibbs in a Lions camp, the multiple arrivals suggested that the batterings on the training ground and on the field of play were taking a heavy toll. This was an expeditionary force falling apart.

That feeling was compounded the next morning when the Wallabies held a press conference at the Pacific Bay to announce their squad of twenty-two for the first Test. They did not name the starting fifteen. That would be done by 'hard copy' – a piece of paper to you and me – at noon the following day. Today, in a large marquee close to the starter's hut on the par-three course, they wheeled out no fewer than fourteen of the twenty-two players. We were most welcome to talk to them for as long as we wished, within reason. The players sat on top table, immaculately groomed and honed and very green and gold in their Wallabies gear. As Rod Macqueen reiterated his line that they had the utmost respect for the Lions, they nodded respectfully. When he repeated his opinion, first made public the day after the game against the Waratahs, that in the Test series sanity would prevail, they all nodded sanely and prevailingly.

By now, just up the road in Opal Cove, the Lions management were turning down all requests to do one-on-one interviews with the press. The Wallabies were presenting themselves as this well-oiled, self-assured and entirely hospitable human machine; the Lions were limping, fighting and putting up the shutters.

Accepting the kind invitation from Djuro Sen, the Wallabies' media manager, to interview at will, I went up to a slightly rotund figure I thought I knew well. 'Hello Mark,' I said, certain that this was the great Mark Ella, the former Wallaby fly half who was now running the marketing campaign for Bundaberg – 'Bundy' – Rum, the sponsors of the tour and the Test series. Why shouldn't he be here? If Campo could do television why couldn't Mark do tents?

If anybody should know Mark Ella, it should be the Welsh player whose last act in international rugby was to give him a try-scoring pass. Oh yes, me. Wales–Australia, 1984. Not a good day. Reminders of it were stalking me. There was a photo in Le Kiosk restaurant on Shelley Beach in Manly of the push-over try they scored. Mercifully I was just out of frame, but there was no escaping my central role in the incident that brought the final curtain down on the game. In the closing moments I turned and threw the ball with the grace of a baby giraffe on ice into the arms of Mark Ella. And off he ran. And down I stayed, with my nose in the musty soil of the old Arms Park . . .

Look, they were a Grand Slam set of magi. It was a pass ahead of its time . . .

'Hello, Mark,' I said.

'Not Mark. Glen,' said the Ella brother who was the assistant coach of the Wallabies, with responsibility for the backs.

I tried to squirm out of this gaffe of mistaking one Ella bro for another by asking Glen about the golden days of Randwick when all three of the Ella boys played together under Bob

Dwyer. And wasn't it funny, didn't he think, how Gary was now doing a similar job as Glen, as assistant to Bob with the Waratahs? And how was Mark, by the way? And that old rascal, Bob, for that matter?

I was doing all this when over came Ian Robertson and said, 'How are you, Mark?' I snorted in disgust and walked away as Glen, with infinite patience said, 'Not Mark, mate. Glen.'

That afternoon we were invited to watch the Wallabies train. They all still looked well groomed and honed. But now they also looked very damned hard and efficient. They went into the session at full blast and, just to show this was for real, they managed to inflict a neck injury on David Giffin. Of course, their medical back-up was so meticulous that the second row would be in 100 per cent condition in time for the Test.

The Lions meanwhile had a rare free afternoon. Some of them went to bed, some went whale-watching and some went jogging. Jogging? Only the maniacs, like Neil Back. Most of the players were on medical report. So many, in fact, that the press were primed to receive at 4.30 p.m. a more precise update from Dr James Robson on who was down with what and when we might expect to see them in action again.

At 4.30 there was no sign of the doctor. Peter Jackson of the *Daily Mail*, chairman of the Rugby Writers, delivered the news that Robson was detained at the team hotel because there had been a tragedy in the Lions camp. Anton Toia, one of two Australian Rugby Union liaison officers with the party, had suffered a fatal heart attack after diving off the whale-watching boat fifty or so yards offshore and swimming back to the beach. Anton was more than just an ARU liaison officer. For thirty years the former front rower had been humping around the luggage of, and making friends with, every incoming tourist to Australia. He was fifty-four years old. Austin would say later that he had been 'a top man, a quality lad who only wanted to give, not take'. When Peter Jackson delivered the news, Barry Coughlan of the *Irish Examiner*, the slightest fellow in our party, who had been a friend of Anton's at home in Cork and abroad in Australia and who had been out with the big fellow several times in Townsville, nearly collapsed. Anton had stood up, waist-deep in the surf, to wave at the Lions players in the boat. They had waved back. Two minutes later he was face down in the water. Two local surfers hauled him to the beach but he was already dead.

The Lions would request to wear black armbands for the midweek game here in Coffs Harbour against New South Wales Country. There would be a minute's silence before the start of the game. They had lost a friend, their party was full of injured players and this was an outing for those who would not feature in the Tests. The team's spirits must have been low.

This was one of those occasions when David Young came into his own. The midweek team never had the full attention of the coaches. They never had a settled group of players, and they had lost against Australia A. Dai, as midweek captain, kept them going with help from Jason Leonard. The two props had mountains of common sense stored in their large frames. They both had the stiff-necked rigidity that comes with too many hours charging and burrowing in the heaving tonnage of humanity known as the scrum. Their gaits suggested that with their barrel-chests they would like to be able to swing breezily along, but they were locked from the sternum up. They were the wise old gurus of the tour.

Martin Corry was asked to play yet again. He very rarely managed to get a full game for England; here in Australia he couldn't stay off the paddock. Colin Charvis and Martyn Williams were alongside him in the back row. Colin was not particularly happy with his lot. He was playing well and yet he couldn't find a way out of the midweek team into the Saturday side.

There was a similar feeling in the second row. It was rumoured that Jeremy Davidson had already been to see the management to ask what he was doing on tour. Malcolm O'Kelly would write before the tour was over that he wasn't having a whole heap of fulfilment from the touring experience.

Gordon Bulloch kept his council. He was between Dai and

Jason in the front row. Their common sense said, 'Keep your head down and get on with it.'

Austin was at scrum half. He, of course, would not keep his head down or keep his own council. By now he was itching to have a game on the wing. Perhaps he knew Rob Howley was very much the number one scrum half. He certainly wanted to help Iain Balshaw regain his confidence. He had said it was all about communication in the back three. A wing could sense what was possible and what not when it came to counter-attacking. Austin, with thirty-eight England caps, thought that he could help Iain through his crisis. The fullback was given another chance, one last chance, to find his form.

Ben Cohen was on the right wing again. It seemed to have become his station in life. He had not looked comfortable there as far back as Perth, but instead of being dropped, he was locked there as tight as the vertebrae in Jason Leonard's neck. Neil Jenkins, worried by a knee that swelled every time he practised his kicking and worried in general about life on this tour, was at outside half. Such was life for some in the midweek team.

Scott Gibbs and Tyrone Howe had no grievances. They were happy to be on tour and happy to be straight into the thick of things. Tyrone took the left wing, Scott the centre position inside his partner with both Swansea and Wales, Mark Taylor.

The Tuesday game against the New South Wales Country Cockatoos was slightly different from all the others in that it was played at three o'clock in the afternoon. Perhaps this was in order to leave the night free for a wild time at the Penthouse Terrace in Orlando Street, Coffs Harbour's brothel that had taken out a full-page advertisement in the match programme. 'Enquire about our new discreet private entrance,' ran the text. All the other matches on tour were night games under flood-lights; this was to be played in full sunshine at the Coffs Harbour International Sports Stadium, a grand name for a quaint little multi-purpose bowl out of town beyond the airport. A handful under ten thousand spectators packed themselves around one side and two ends of the pitch. The far side had a bank, which was an ideal place from which to watch a game of Aussie Rules but was so far from the rugby action that only trained astronomers sat there.

The NSW Cockatoos were made up of players from all over the vast rural areas of the state. Amateurs from clubs like Wollongong, Woonoona, Avoca, Tamworth, Orange, Crookwell, Camden, Maitland, Campbelltown and Newcastle had come together, as they had been doing since 1946, to have their hour on the big stage. 'Playing for the Country Cockatoos is all about pride,' their captain, Bernie Klasen would say after the game. 'Last night John Eales came and gave us our jumpers [shirts] and told us the whole of Australia was behind us. That was great, even if the big fellah is a Queenslander. We sang the national anthem in the sheds and a few of the guys had tears in their eyes.'

Would the Cockatoos turn out to be a redneck handful against the tourists, or mere enthusiasts happy to keep the score respectable, to under a hundred? They turned out to be a team in the middle. They leaked nearly fifty points but went hard at the Lions from start to finish, making life difficult for the professional tourists, at the scrummage in particular.

I was sitting in the front row of the stand. There was no room in the small grandstand for a conventional press box and we were arranged in rows at ground level. The sound of the big tackles and the thudding of shoulder into soft tissue could be clearly heard.

I was sitting next to the duty doctor, Dr Michael Ridley. He did not have to do any of the hands-on treatment of the players, but was simply there to double-check that the team doctors, James Robson for the Lions and Arthur Bosanquet for the Cockatoos, did not allow injured players who should be withdrawn to resume playing. What this meant was that he could sit back and enjoy the game. And have a chat.

He had come to Australia forty years ago. Having recently qualified as a doctor at University College Hospital in London he had been among the last intake for National Service in Britain. As a doctor, rather than go into the army, he could opt to work for two years in Australia. He went to rural Victoria and never came home. For the past thirty-seven years he had been in Coffs Harbour.

Scott Gibbs, making an immediate and forceful impact in the centre, broke clear and linked with the back row, one after the other. Martin Corry was having another outstanding game, closely followed by Colin Charvis and Martyn Williams. For all three this performance would be important. From the ruck they set up, Ben Cohen scored in the corner.

Dr Michael was a rural general practitioner with a specialist interest in gastroenterology, but he was also president of the Australian Medical Association (NSW). He had to deal with politicians. 'I give them hell,' he said. 'It's the same the world over. They try to give you their smooth talk and then they try to give you less money. I treat them all the same, as a pack of rogues. I don't suppose they like me much either. But what do we want, to end up with a health service like yours? Most of the guys who qualified at the same time as me and stayed in Britain are either dead or they've retired, fed up.'

Colin Charvis burst into the three-quarter line and powered through three tackles to score. Graham Henry had conceded that the Welsh wing forward had a point about not being given much of a chance in the Saturday side, but that was how things sometimes went on short tours. Charvis was remaking his point by deed.

Scott Gibbs scored five minutes later. An intricate, flowing series of passes out of the tackle, started and finished by the centre, created the try of the game.

A woman came up to Michael and said she'd been told it would be OK to come and see him in surgery at 8.30 the next day. Michael said that would be fine. He was doing a vasectomy at eight, but should be done by half past.

Tyrone Howe went close to the line. The Ulsterman's first contribution had been to receive the ball while he was a yard and a half in touch. 'Hardly an auspicious start,' he would say later. Now he was in play on all counts. He set up a ruck, Scott Gibbs ran to the blind side, attracted the cover and Austin darted over.

'Hardly very difficult,' would be Austin's assessment. He was more pleased with his try-saving tackle on one of their wings. 'I surprised him a bit. I grabbed him by the collar and hauled him back as he was diving for the line. I was pleased with that.'

A player from the Under-19 curtain-raiser came and showed Michael a deep gash above his eyebrow. 'Don't say I have to work,' said the doctor. 'Don't worry,' said the nurse, 'I'll sort him out.' And away they went to clean and dress the wound.

David Young scored early in the second half. Michael had told me about his two replacement hips – thanks to too many years of opening the bowling in rural NSW cricket – and I think we were back on the subject of vasectomies when the Welsh prop and midweek captain went over. We both missed it. There must be a metaphor in there somewhere. A few minutes later Malcolm O'Kelly sent out one of his rather classical long miss-passes and Ben Cohen was running away for his second try.

And that was the end of the action. The game wandered along for another half-hour without going anywhere. It had certainly gone nowhere for Iain Balshaw. He had produced another faltering performance. The fullback, who could be so enlightening with his audacious running, continued to be all over the shop on tour. It was a relief when the referee, who had not let things flow, blew up for full time. Michael and I shook hands. He wished us all the best for the rest of the tour and away he went.

Amazingly – and Donal had to check his notebook to confirm it was true – there were no injuries to report at the press conference afterwards. This was held in a tent outside the ground, in a compound shared with the police. The state constabulary had not exactly had a busy afternoon, but there had been the usual bunch of pitch-invaders to deal with. As the press gathered in their compound the police were cautioning a typical list of fans sporting Batman capes or with the Union flag painted on their face.

Pitch-invading was not the done thing in Australia. The newspapers at this time were carrying long reports on the crowd invasions at the one-day cricket matches in England, and in particular on the can of beer thrown at Michael Bevan after

Australia's victory over Pakistan in the final. Such disturbances were frowned upon, and spectators were warned at all rugby games that running onto the field of play would incur a hefty fine. This had not stopped one spectator at the Coffs Harbour game from putting on a bit of a show. He had not invaded the pitch, as such, but had stripped behind the goal and, stark naked, had climbed up a cherry-picker hoist to join a television cameraman on his rostrum. Fox Sport's pictures may have shaken for a moment. The crowd cheered as the streaker held his arms aloft. They cheered even more as the cherry-picker was lowered to the ground. And then they booed as the man's hands were cuffed behind his back and he was led away, even more fully exposed. There was a lot of banter about his cockatoo.

The press conference had a sideshow, too. It was stolen by Dorian West, the replacement hooker, who had not even been required to go on the field. He was wheeled out with the other newcomers, Tyrone Howe, David Wallace and Scott Gibbs. And Gordon Bulloch, although the Scottish hooker was hardly a newcomer by now. Scott had been at home when the call came from Australia. The Irish players had been on their way to Poland, of all places, to a training camp there. David Wallace had done an about-turn in Copenhagen.

Where had Dorian been? 'I'd just landed in Minorca with the wife and kids,' he said. 'It must have been about six o'clock in the evening. I drove them to this villa we'd booked and by eight o'clock I was back on a plane, first to Frankfurt, then Australia. I was still in my sandals and shorts.'

And what had Mrs West thought of all this?

'I think she was a bit upset,' said deadpan Dorian. The Leicester Tigers now had five Lions.

The next press conference promised fewer chuckles. The following morning, Wednesday, the Lions announced their team for the first Test at the Gabba in Brisbane. It was pouring with rain as we headed from Pacific Bay to Opal Cove. The pneumatic drills had started up at seven o'clock. Australia had already announced their team. There were no real surprises there.

Nathan Grey was in the centre instead of Elton Flatley; Owen Finegan had stepped in for Matt Cockbain in the back row. Rod Macqueen had tweaked the Wallabies to give them more muscle.

The Lions, of course, did have an injury to announce after all. Typical. Neil Back's rib injury was going to keep him out of the first Test. We were tempted to ask, 'What rib injury?' but were too engrossed in how the Lions would re-jig their back row to accommodate the loss of the wing forward who was supposed to have been going head-to-head with the Wallaby sensation, George Smith.

Richard Hill was to replace Neil on the open side. Martin Corry was to win a Test place on the blind side. Martin had gone from being bridesmaid in the England camp to being handed the bouquet in Brisbane. Scott Quinnell was at number eight.

The other surprise was that Tom Smith was named at loose-head prop instead of Darren Morris. Word had been circulating all week that the Lions coaches felt that in the match against the Waratahs, when the game had exploded and the brawling was at its most unrestrained, Darren had gone missing. This had surprised us. What, he was going to lose his place because he had shown restraint? Or was it that he wasn't hard enough? I thought of my three Bristol boys in Manly and hoped I would not see them again.

It was another decision taken with chilling abruptness, and appeared to offer a glimpse into how the Lions were expected to play. They had lost their chaser of the ball going wide; they had opted for tightness. I still couldn't believe Darren Morris had failed some sort of courage test, but it was great news for Tom Smith, one of the stars of the 1997 tour to South Africa.

Tom had started slowly in Australia. After his first game in Townsville, the statistics had been thrown around that his tackle count had been zero and his ball-carrying count one. Or was it the other way round? He had been improving with every game, which in mathematical terms wasn't too difficult. No, that was unfair, because anyone with an ounce of knowledge about front-row play – and that wouldn't include me – would tell you that there was still a massive amount to the prop's art that wasn't covered by wretched statistics. Although Tom himself had been saying in the week that perhaps his chances of being selected for the first Test had vanished.

Keith Wood was declared fit and took his place in the middle of Tom and Phil Vickery. Behind this front row were the all-important colossi of Martin Johnson and Danny Grewcock in the second. If ever Johnson were injured, we might as well all pack up and go home.

The front five was formidable, the back row powerful, if not the most rapid on the planet. This was the pack whose efforts would directly determine whether the game was won or lost. That was an age-old adage, but rarely had a pack of forwards borne so much responsibility.

In the three-quarters Iain Balshaw was left on the bench. Matt Perry was to play at full back. This was sure-fire confirmation that this was to be a Test played without high risk. An even higher risk would have been to select Iain. The ever-analytical Wallabies might just have made a target of him. As in, unleash hell on him. Perhaps Graham Henry was full of compassion, after all. The entirely dependable Dafydd James was chosen on the right wing. Jason Robinson was entrusted with the left wing position. By now, such was his form that he was hardly considered a gamble.

Rob Henderson was selected at inside centre. Again, given his form on tour, it did not trigger any alarm bells to see Rob there, despite the injuries to the original front-runners for the number twelve shirt, Mike Catt and Will Greenwood. His partner in the centre was to be Brian O'Driscoll. No surprise at all there. He had risen sharply from his suspect position at fullback in Perth to assume a place of authority at outside centre.

Rob Howley and Jonny Wilkinson were the straightforward choices at halfback. Simple selections, but these were the key characters, with the all-consuming and desperately difficult task of containing their opposite numbers, George Gregan and Stephen Larkham.

After the team announcement the Test players plus the re-

placements were available for interviews. Numbers correspond-
ing with their shirts were placed on tables, and in drifted the
chosen twenty-two. Austin was number twenty-one, and was to
share a table with number twenty, Matt Dawson. Austin was on
the bench as the second-string outside half now. Matt would
cover Rob Howley. I had to talk to Austin, but I also needed to
garner some quotes from Scott Quinnell for an *Observer* feature
on the number eight being written from home.

I offered Austin congratulations on his place in the Test squad.
He scoffed them aside. He raged against Graham Henry: 'He's
the Emperor Ming. He never talks to anyone, certainly not me.
Not even the other coaches. Everything is his decision.' I said
that Graham Henry was very complimentary about him in
public. He paused for a second and then scoffed again. 'What
am I? I came as a scrum half, now I'm a fly half. What about
wing? Thirty-eight Test selections and not even a look-in.'

Scott was delighted to be back in the frame having missed the
Tests in South Africa through injury. 'It's unbelievable,' he said,
'It's just outstanding for me. I had a few ghosts to lay after South
Africa.'

Austin criticised the lack of attention given to the midweek
team. 'Do you know what we did on Monday by way of getting
ready for Tuesday? We were told we were the Wallabies, and we
had to do Aussie moves against the Test team. I was George
Gregan. The only good thing was that we gave them a good
dicking.'

Scott said he was playing well because his family was happy.
He had enjoyed his time in Wigan, in rugby league, but on his
return to union he had never settled in London and had not
really performed for Richmond. Now that he was back in his
home town, Llanelli, everything was going well.

Austin said his buttock was bad, that Jeremy Davidson had
pulled the chair from underneath him at the team meeting. He
now called Jeremy 'Dangerous Brian'. He said he had had an
almighty row with the fourth official at Coffs Harbour: 'Some
little dickhead who tried to stop Richard Hill bringing on water
for the players. I told him he was clean off his head. It was

twenty-five degrees out there. He said if I continued to argue he'd report me to the referee. I said I'd save him the bother. I went up to this bloke who was ruining the game and told him he was a cheat. He ignored me.'

Scott hadn't really changed anything about his game. Perhaps he was a bit fitter nowadays, but so was everyone else. He still weighed the same as always, some eighteen and a half stone. He knew he had a big job ahead, to make the hard yards from the scrum and from mauls and restarts. 'I know I have this low centre of gravity. It sort of runs in the family. Short legs, we call it. But no, I don't think too much about body angles or anything. I just pick up and go.'

Austin didn't approve of the strategy for the Test. 'I said from the start that we would have to do something special. Well, we're not. It's going to be these two massive defences hammering shit out of each other. Whoever comes out less damaged will pinch the result.'

Scott said he was sorry Lawrence had been injured. The camp needed internal competition to keep everybody sharp and on his toes. It was no relief to him to know that a rival was out of the reckoning. 'If Lawrence had been playing well, he might have got the nod. If I was playing well, it might be me. Well, it's turned out that it's me. I'm delighted, but the team comes first.'

Austin said there was trouble brewing in the camp. 'Everybody is so pissed off with this tour. It's meant to be the chance of a lifetime. Well, it's not and there's going to be a mutiny. I hate this tour. I hate it.'

Scott said thank you as I wished him good luck.

I left Austin as he was starting to jest with Matt Dawson about the analogy of two walls running into each other. Matt thought it would be better if they were walls on wheels. I think Austin felt a bit better having at least got something off his chest.

At the airport in Coffs Harbour I met Scott Gibbs. He was in bubbling form. For such an abrasive centre Scott was softly spoken, professorial behind his specs. I said it might have been one of the stories of the tour if he had pitched up, had a run-out against the Cockatoos and been put straight into the Test team. No, he didn't think he could possibly have been selected. And if the Lions won, he wouldn't make the second. But who could tell what might happen before the third?

He asked me if I had seen the documentary on him that BBC Wales had just transmitted. I said that before leaving for Australia I had talked about the project with Dylan Richards, the producer, but had not seen the finished piece. Dylan would have done a good job, because Scott was a fine subject, a rugby player who had a heap of interests outside rugby. He loved New York; Dylan had taken him there. They had done jazz clubs. I wondered whether having so many pursuits extraneous to rugby would have counted against Scott in the selection process for a tour as ascetic as this. I asked him if he was happy with the finished documentary. He said that he was not a great television viewer, but he had watched it four or five times. Just to make sure he hadn't revealed too much of himself. They really should have picked him in the first place.

An hour later the Lions left the strange plastic paradise of Coffs Harbour and headed for Brisbane and the realities of the first Test.

11

Back to Brisbane

Brisbane was on sporting fire. On Friday night there was to be an Aussie Rules showdown at the Brisbane Cricket Ground in Woolloongabba, universally known as the Gabba, between the Brisbane Lions and Hawthorn of Melbourne. As soon as that game was done, and the local Lions had – sweet omen? – won, the Gabba was to have its lines repainted and its posts reconfigured for the first Test between the Lions of rugby union and the Wallabies.

They were playing for the Tom Richards Cup, made of Waterford crystal and named after a wonderful character who was born in Australia in 1882 but who went to work in the goldmines of South Africa at the age of twenty-three. Richards followed the 1906 Springboks on their tour to England and ended up playing against them for Gloucestershire. He went back to Australia and won a place on the first Wallaby tour of 1908, to Britain, only to return to South Africa afterwards.

When the Lions toured South Africa in 1910 they were soon looking for replacements. Because of his loose Gloucestershire connection, Richards qualified in a precursor-to-Grannygate sort of way. He remains the only Australian national to play for the Lions, appearing in two Tests against the Springboks. Having gone back to Australia and been on a Wallaby tour to the USA, he then went to France via England and played for Biarritz before the First World War. In 1914 he enlisted, was one of the first on to the beaches at Gallipoli, served on the Western Front in France and was awarded the Military Cross. He died in Brisbane in 1935 of tuberculosis, saying that 'the gas I swallowed during the war is beating me down slowly.' Follow that.

Rugby league would have to try. Union Saturday would become league Sunday. The third night of sport would be played at the ANZ, the stadium built for the 1982 Commonwealth Games and now reserved for State of Origin III, the decider of the interstate series between Queensland and New South Wales. The Cane Toads and the Cockroaches.

If this had been Melbourne, the Aussie Rules game would have held sway. In Sydney the rugby league would have been making all the headlines. As it would in Brisbane in any normal year. I had been in the capital of Queensland once before when the State of Origin coincided with a rugby union Test, and had been to promotional functions in city-centre shopping malls. Union was only offering Australia against England on the Tour from Hell, but it was still a Test match. The league fans had outnumbered union followers two hundred to one.

But this was not any normal year. Brisbane was glowing red. If the numbers of Lions supporters had been swelling before the game against Queensland at Ballymore, now the city was about to burst. To walk down the pedestrianised Queen Street was to try to part a sea of replica shirts. Hoteliers and members of the Chamber of Commerce had totted up their figures and estimated that there were twenty thousand fans from overseas in town. Brisbane was, they guessed, to benefit from a spending spree of ten million dollars.

We were twelve thousand miles from home, but it felt like Dublin and Twickenham and Murrayfield and Cardiff on match day. But especially Cardiff. If Gullivers, the largest of the English tour operators, were shipping in four thousand supporters, three thousand were from Wales.

At the same time as we arrived in Brisbane from Coffs Harbour, Fairwater RFC of Cardiff were being unloaded not so fresh from their longer-haul flight from London. There, too, in Arrivals were the slightly more polished singers of the Lions

Male Voice Choir. When you went by name of Melody Music you could not step off the plane wrecked.

The next day I found myself on one of the city ferries that go upstream and downstream, criss-crossing the Brisbane River from landing stage to landing stage. I was talking to a couple of locals who confessed that they had never been on the ferry before, even though they had lived in the city all their lives. But they would do it again because it seemed a good way to meet people. The forty other passengers were all Lions fans. I left the couple starting up a conversation with a man sporting a beard, glasses, sandals and a jumper with 'Huddersfield Choir' on the breast. He was pulling out a giant map of the city: 'Now, you couldn't just pinpoint for me exactly where that would be, where she's buried, could you . . . ?'

Back in the city centre I was waiting at some traffic lights when a large group on hired bicycles pulled up. 'All right, Ed butt?' they said. And for fifteen seconds or so we talked about the weather back home. Then the funny bloop-bloop-bloop started, the sound that told pedestrians it was safe to cross, and we were going our separate ways.

I was heading back to the Novotel on Creek Street when I passed St Andrew's Uniting Church. Outside, Dr Haydn James was handing out leaflets for the concert to be given that night in said church by the Lions Male Voice Choir, no less. No wonder they hadn't been on the lash on the plane. I said to the choirmaster that I'd do my best to attend. But, to be honest, male voice choirs were not my bag.

I was made what we loosely called choirmaster of the 1980 Wales B trip to the USA and Canada. Much against the expectations of our hosts, the team toured the entire North American continent without hitting a single note. It was one of the low points of my playing career, nearly as bad as being sent off, on that same tour, in Victoria, Vancouver Island, while playing against British Columbia. Personally I'd say it was, like asking me to lead the team in song, a case of mistaken identity.

The next day the Lions held a press conference at the Sheraton. For the first time the Australian media nearly outnumbered

us. Donal Lenihan raised an eyebrow and said how nice it was to
see them there. And spent the next five minutes fending off all the
usual questions: did the Lions think it might blow up into a
brawl? Having been pursued around Australia by allegations
that they were cheats and thugs, what were the Lions going to
bring to the Test match?

With a watchful world-weariness Donal and Martin Johnson
deflected the missiles. 'It's a Test match against the best team in the
world,' said Martin. 'There won't be time to think of anything
other than your own job.' He didn't elucidate what his job might
be. If it included taking out John Eales at the first opportunity, the
question would have been valid. But, of course, the captain's job,
the team's job, as he and they had always said, was to play rugby.

'We're here to play rugby,' added Donal for the three hun-
dredth time on tour.

Only Graham Henry returned a question with a bit of top-
spin. 'Coach Henry,' a voice came at him from the floor, 'it's
been said that your Lions are the most unfriendly set of tourists
ever. In fact, they're known over here as the Grumpy Lions.
What is your response to that?'

'Is that right?' said Graham, in his trademark way, which gave
him a moment to collect his thoughts. 'I think it's a load of
rubbish. Is that grumpy enough for you?'

If the newspapers of Australia were having trouble inciting the
Lions to come out with an inflammatory quote, then it was
about to go off elsewhere. In the British press. All the stresses and
strains and disappointments and sheer drudgery of the tour for a
group expected to train and train with no greater hope than to be
cannon-fodder for the Test team burst into print through the
vehicle of one player's diary.

It wasn't Austin's. I had managed to keep my discipline and
continued to filter out the more outrageous of his comments. I
had come to the conclusion that if I wasn't exactly playing the
role of confessor to Austin, then at least I was his censor. He
ranted at me and felt better immediately. And off he would go,
back to the world of non-stop training and preparation for

match day. He was the only player who had been selected either in the first-up team or on the replacements' bench for every game. Besides, I had the feeling, despite what he had said in Coffs Harbour, that perhaps it wasn't the best time – in the Friday *Guardian* before the Saturday Test – to let him let rip, as it were. I didn't think it was the moment to let the world know that Austin called Graham Henry the Emperor Ming.

Matthew Dawson thought otherwise. He had been at Austin's table after the team was announced. He had listened to, and shared in, the venting of frustration. Perhaps he thought it was common currency and now was the time to go public. Throughout the tour Matt had been keeping a handwritten diary for the *Daily Telegraph*. I saw him hand his latest instalment to Mick Cleary, the paper's rugby correspondent.

Mick read it, blinked, wrote it up and handed it back to Matt to be checked. The paragraphs came back again with a tick against each one. Off went the diary to appear in the *Telegraph* on the morning of the match. It revealed the seething discontent in the camp, the lack of respect for Graham Henry, the unremitting workload and the gathering mutiny. Players had threatened to leave the tour. I was still a bit worried about the trigger for all this. But no, Mick said, the trouble dated back way beyond Coffs Harbour.

The Dawson Diary coincided with the arrival overnight of an e-mail on the sports desks of all the British papers. The e-mail had no signature but purported to come from within the Lions camp. It spelt out in even stronger terms than the diary the air of mutiny and the breakdown in trust and respect between players and coaches. Brian Oliver at the *Observer* rang me first thing Saturday morning his time – that was 5.30 p.m. in Brisbane, an hour and a half before the game – and asked what I thought of it. I said everything depended on the result. If the Lions won, any sedition would be silenced. By the natural processes of celebration, that is, rather than a squad of hit-men. The stories were obviously penned by a person or persons who believed the Lions could not win. If they lost, then we would have a monster of a story on our hands.

The pessimistic mood seemed to have spread. The supporters were streaming out of Queen Street, down to the river, towards the bridge that led to the Gabba. They were prepared to give it their all, but the prevailing mood among them suggested that they, too, believed that their team would lose: too many injuries, too many indifferent passages of play late in games, too many sour rumours. The A result had hurt; the Waratahs had taken a heavy toll. The Wallabies, the world champions, would be too strong.

We arrived at the Gabba. The back of the stand above Gate 5 hung out over Vulture Street. Quite menacing really – or so it seemed. The mood was getting to me. I reminded myself that both Brian Oliver and Roger Alton, the editor himself of the *Observer*, had asked me the day before for a sensible prediction. This had been serious. They both liked a flutter and wanted to know on whom to stake their money.

Almost at the same time I had done an interview with Talk Sport Radio of New Zealand. I had weighed up the odds: the resilience of the spirit of the likes of Martin Johnson and Richard Hill against, well, everything stacked against them. To both the office in London and the listeners of New Zealand I had said the Lions would win. But I had gulped as I said it.

I went round to the back of the stadium, to try to record some 'atmosphere' for the Radio 4 programme. I found myself isolated. The sea of Lions red, flecked with Wallaby green and gold, had melted away. I entered a compound full of leotards and dinner jackets. Tuxedos and Lycra as far as the eye could see. Surreal. This was the warm-up area for the pre-match entertainers. The Lions Male Voice Choir were stretching their tonsils in one corner, a Brisbane Barbers Shop ensemble were in full voice in another. Dancers high-stepped here, cheerleaders tumbled there. Singing might not be my bag, but when Dr Haydn James interrupted his last-minute rehearsal and told me not to worry, that the Lions would be fine, I could have hugged him.

Inside the ground, the press were divided into two: half went up to the press box on level two of the three-tiered Gabba, half down to level one. The view from the press box was good, but there was a complete lack of sound. We were separated from the outside world by glass off which an anti-tank shell would bounce. Silent rugby. Even more surreal.

I went downstairs to the overspill area. As I stepped out into the open air I hit a wall of sound: 'Lions, Lions, Lions.' It was hardly an award-winning verse, but it generated the tingle that can go with sport on the grand scale. Southern hemisphere crowds did not produce an atmosphere? The theory was being shredded.

In fact, the noise was coming from the northern hordes. The sea of supporters from Queen Street had crossed the river and had grown again. Had doubled, trebled in size. The Gabba was a red-hot crucible. 'I'd rather be a Lion than a 'roo' rang out. Simon and Garfunkle.

Martin Johnson and John Eales came out to toss the coin. The Lions captain went back to the changing room and told the team that they were playing at home.

The sound system broke down for much of the pre-match entertainment, which probably spoilt part of the night for the Lions Male Voice Choir. No amplification was required when Martin Johnson led his team into the arena. They appeared through a tunnel a hundred metres distant from the Wallabies' entrance. The public address system came back to life for 'Advance Australia Fair'. There was Aussie support here after all.

The game of abattoir-chess began. This was going to be an opening session of jarring collision, of analysis and watchful probing. The ball stayed in the air for a long time as it was punted back and forth between Stephen Larkham and Matt Perry. Martin Johnson took responsibility for the first line-out, called for the ball to be thrown to himself and won it cleanly.

And then watchful probing was poked in the eye. Danny Grewcock, who had matched his captain and second-row partner blow for blow – as it were – throughout the tour, won a line-out and delivered it from the top of his leap to scrum half Robert Howley. For the three-quarters this was the best ball in the business: quick possession that allowed them to maximise the twenty-metre gap between their opponents and themselves.

Brian O'Driscoll at centre went for a little dart on the outside, made it halfway through and sent an inside pass over his shoulder. Rob Howley picked it off his toes. Two passes later, the ball was in the hands of Jason Robinson. The one place where the former rugby league player might not be at ease was tight against the touchline. Something in his league bones told him that the touchline was taboo. The Wallaby fullback, Chris Latham, offered the wing the outside channel. The invitation was there: to beat me you have to beat the taboo. Jason did not hesitate. He stepped in and then out towards touch. The fullback dived but the wing was gone, flirting with the out-of-bounds but then clear. The Lions had unstitched the best defence in the world straight from set-piece, when the line of tacklers was at its most organised. Giving the ball to Jason Robinson after two minutes forty-eight seconds probably had not featured that high on the coach's list of tactical probes, but it was a stroke of genius.

The half-dart by Brian O'Driscoll had been as revealing as the finish by Jason Robinson. This was more in keeping with the master-plan. The Wallabies were vulnerable in midfield. Stephen Larkham was an expert reader of the game when in possession. And now that he had had laser surgery on his eyes, enabling him to discern the posts at the far end as something sharper than an H-shaped fuzz, he was feared as the play-maker who might make the Lions suffer. But he was targeted now as a defensive weak link. Moreover, Brian O'Driscoll seemed to have the edge, as he had done against Queensland on the Lions' first visit to Brisbane, over Daniel Herbert. And there was even more encouragement, because if George Smith was a flyer in the Wallaby back row, then there was not quite as much quick-twitch agility in the shapes of Toutai Kefu at number eight and Owen Finegan on the blind side.

Rob Henderson had been one of the surprise stars of the tour. From day one in Perth he had combined the thundering runs, for which he was well known at Wasps and with Ireland, with a kicking game from hand that nobody suspected he had in his armoury. He had been ferocious in the tackle and, oh yes, he had also revealed a sprinter's turn of pace to run in and contribute to any biff going. 'Going the biff' was a favourite Aussie phrase for brawling, and apparently a favourite pastime of Rob's. In short, he fitted in. Not long after Jason Robinson's try, Rob made a clean break in midfield. He simply cut through, ran towards the fullback and prepared to deliver the final pass to Brian O'Driscoll who had tracked his partner's steps and looped around him to be available for the run-in.

Rob passed. And Joe Roff intercepted. The Wallaby wing had gambled on the pass and it had paid off. It meant that the Lions, instead of sprinting upfield, were suddenly doing an about-turn and haring back to save their own line. The situation was saved by Jonny Wilkinson. The outside half covered Roff's kick ahead and launched a counterattack that was to feature Scott Quinnell and Keith Wood on the charge. It ended with a chip by Brian O'Driscoll, which Andrew Walker, the Wallaby right wing, carried over his own line for a scrum five. The game was supposed to be garrotte-tight. Instead, it was swaying back and forth in a frenzy of running.

The Lions had to come away with something to show for this five-metre position. They returned empty-handed. The scrum was re-set, once, twice, and then a back-row move led only to a penalty, awarded against Phil Vickery for entering a ruck from the side. It was a warning. The Lions had struggled to come to terms with what the southern hemisphere referees would allow at the tackle area. Andre Watson of South Africa did not seem to mind an immediate chicken-scratch for the ball among the early arrivals at the breakdown. But he was to be harsh on any later arrivals hitting the loose formation at anything other than a precise right angle to a line drawn straight across the field.

The Wallabies cleared their lines. It was a missed chance. And soon Andrew Walker was kicking a penalty that reduced the gap to two points. Once again the referee had objected to the angle of entry at a ruck. It was one of the reasons why rugby, for all its dramas and intrigue, might never win a wider audience. So much appealing wildness had to be allied to so much esoteric precision.

The kickers were not settling into their roles. Andrew Walker missed an easy penalty attempt, after another offence at the ruck, that would have put the Wallabies in the lead. Jonny Wilkinson had missed the conversion of the try, and had also missed with his first penalty. Now he hit the top of the post with his second, the ball coming down vertically on the upright and bouncing off-line. None of the Lions kickers was particularly at ease with the Summit ball used in Australia.

Jonny finally found the target. It wasn't just a three-point penalty but the two-point addition to the Lions' second try. A scrum on the right-hand side went even further right up the blind side towards the far touchline, the opposite side of the field from Jason Robinson's orthodox position on the left wing. But on the shoulder of Brian O'Driscoll, whose own run from outside centre to the blind side had been daring enough to see him past Owen Finegan, there he was. Centre fed wing. Jason drew a defender and released Dafydd James. For the second time, Chris Latham was diving at thin air. From the touchline, which counted as pretty good therapy for a kicker yet to find his range, Jonny sent the ball clean through the posts.

There was just one last incident in the first half. Scott Quinnell was penalised for a high tackle on a player yet to receive the ball. A sort of double penalty that evoked all those accusations about the Lions being over-vigorous off the ball and prone to acts of foul play. It was, however, but a faint echo of the build-up to the Test. Andre Watson lectured Quinnell paternally rather than sternly. And Andrew Walker missed the kick. At half-time the Lions were nine points ahead.

Both sides changed their fullback at half-time, the Lions through injury, the Wallabies through unease at the tackling of their last line of defence and at their inability to kick goals. On came Iain Balshaw for Matt Perry, who had a groin strain, and on came Matthew Burke for Chris Latham.

The Wallabies' new rearmost defender had barely taken up his post when he was called upon to make his first tackle. Straight from the start of the second period, a kick-off claimed by Danny Grewcock. The Lions swept downfield in a series of handling movements and hit the Wallabies hard again in midfield. That man, Brian O'Driscoll. The centre, whose eyesight in normal life was anything but sharp, spotted a gap and surged through it. Matt Burke raced up, a model of aggressive defence. Brian danced to the left and another fullback was left clutching at mist. The cover defence came at the Irish centre, who had stumbled slightly on breaking the fullback's tackle, from three angles. Brian recovered his step and won the sprint for the line.

Five minutes later, as if he hadn't done enough, Brian was off again, breaking through, initiating a move that led to a penalty kicked by Jonny Wilkinson. And five minutes after that, the game was won. Martin Corry, a rock on the blind side to complement Scott Quinnell's running from number eight and Richard Hill's tackling on the open side, won a line-out, and the Lions – no surprises now – hit hard in the centre. Rob Henderson's run was eventually stopped by John Eales, still making covering tackles a decade after he rewrote the way the second-row game could be played at the 1991 World Cup. But the momentum could not be stopped. Rob Howley ran laterally to allow Iain Balshaw to run hard and straight onto his pass. The replacement fullback fell just short of the line. Scott Quinnell arrived, picked up and dived over. And over went the conversion. The Lions had scored four tries; they led 29–3 with half an hour to go. The contest was over.

It could not have been going worse for Australia. The fourth try left behind it a trail of injuries. Hooker Jeremy Paul was taken off on a stretcher with a knee injury that would rule him out for the rest of the season. Stephen Larkham walked off at the same time holding his elbow, to be replaced by Elton Flatley.

It appeared that the Lions would take full advantage. Rob Howley intercepted a pass and kicked downfield. Jason Robinson set off in pursuit. The Wallabies only just managed to scramble back.

But then the game took one final turn. The result was so little in doubt that the Wallabies did not bother to kick for goal now.

They kicked to the corner and tried to score tries. To see them reduced to that, with twenty-five minutes remaining, was so improbable that a hush settled on the Gabba. But the twist was that in this muted final period, the power of the Lions declined, as if they were directly attached to the volume control of their supporters.

And as the victors began to lose their urgency and their discipline, so Australia began to assert themselves. Matt Burke dived over in the corner, the try only disallowed because video replays confirmed that Jason Robinson had managed to force him into touch. Andre Watson began to blow the life out of the Lions at the breakdown. His repeated warnings would eventually see first Martin Corry, then Phil Vickery, sent to the sin-bin for persistent infringements at the ruck. Toutai Kefu had a try disallowed for crossing in midfield. Colin Charvis came off the bench and played with his customary forcefulness, except that he overdid a piece of 'clearing' at the ruck and kneed prop Nick Stiles. The Welsh wing forward would later be cited by the independent commissioner and banned for two games. It looked a bit harsh. 'Maybe,' said Colin later, 'but he could have done me for a lot of other stuff.'

While Martin Corry was absent, the Wallabies scored. Andrew Walker, the failed kicker, gave a glimpse of how lethal he could be as a runner by slicing through from thirty metres. Nathan Grey combined with Joe Roff to score a second try four minutes later. It would all have been a bit alarming had not the Lions enjoyed a cushion of twenty-six points. And had not Keith Wood broken the tension with a little light relief with two minutes to go.

The Irish hooker, in accordance with a dream he had apparently had the previous May, scooped up the ball in the middle of the pitch and attempted a drop goal. It landed slightly short. Like twenty metres short. But it somehow defused the mini-crisis. Keith had been immense during the establishment of the shock hegemony of the tourists. His tackling, like Phil Vickery's, was one of the talking points of the night. As were the power of the centres, the physical dominance of the second rows, the balance of the back row, the authority of the halfbacks and the brilliance of Jason Robinson, not forgetting the silent acceptance of a heavy payload by Dafydd James and Tom Smith. Everybody had played his part. It took a failed drop goal by the bald hooker to remind us that the job had been done a long while back and that there was no reason to panic. Sit back and relax.

Until the second Test. Graham Henry said afterwards how pleased he was. Thus far. Martin Johnson said that the night compared with anything he'd ever achieved in the game. But the job was only half done. A third done.

Then came the inevitable damper. Stephen Jones of the *Sunday Times* asked, in the light of the revelations by Matt Dawson in that morning's *Telegraph*, what the management intended to do with the player. Donal Lenihan must have known it was coming. He said he had not read the article and that he would not be able to comment until he had. He felt the night belonged to the players who had pulled off an unbelievable victory. These were the nights to remember. But might we not forget at the same time that there was a long way to go yet.

Such reticence to embrace a famous victory was wasted on the red army. They swooped down into Vulture Street and poured back towards the city. The Chamber of Commerce had said the invaders were going to spend ten million dollars. Now they would spend twenty. 'Three dollars to the pound, three dollars to the pound . . .' they sang. Mary Hopkin, if my ears didn't deceive me.

And just for the record, on Sunday night Allan 'Alfie' Langer at the age of thirty-four came back from the Warrington Wolves in Cheshire to inspire Queensland to victory in State of Origin III. The Cane Toads of Queensland saw off the Cockroaches of New South Wales. Alfie had done it again, and Queensland took the series 2–1. And with that, Brisbane emptied, its sporting triptych of Rules, union and league, but above all union, over.

12

Canberra, only once

Canberra would be different. Everybody said so. We were going from a city rave in tropical Queensland to a monastic retreat, the nation's capital. Canberra was like that: spacious and chilly. Socially frigid and meteorologically frosty.

On the plane from Brisbane to Canberra early on Sunday morning I sat next to a woman who was on her way to see one of her five children and two of her ten grandchildren. She had three sons and two daughters, all married, all neatly distributed over Oceania – Perth, Adelaide, Canberra, Brisbane and Queenstown in New Zealand – and all neatly blessed with two children. She herself lived in a retirement complex on the Sunshine Coast north of Brisbane and travelled wherever her babysitting services were required next.

'What's Canberra like?' I asked.

'Canberra is . . . Well, Canberra is . . .' she replied and stopped. 'Canberra has good roads,' she concluded.

Normally she drove from Brisbane to Canberra, stopping off at friends' houses along the way. The very long way, that was. 'The roads are good all down the states,' she said, 'but especially as you get towards Canberra. I have a little Mazda, you know. I say to myself that I must be getting near the capital because suddenly I'm up to 140 kph without realising it.'

Canberra did indeed have long, wide roads. And on the Sunday of our arrival they were very empty. Without wishing to push thoroughly democratic Australia into totalitarian comparisons, it was a bit like Bucharest in 1984. Of course, there was no broken-down combine harvester on Northbourne Avenue as there had been on one of Ceaușescu's deserted boulevards, but the empty wideness beneath a wintry blue sky was slightly chilling. Somebody mentioned the Stepford Wives.

These were unfair comparisons. On Sunday night the press regathered in King O'Malley's Irish Bar – not too many of those in Bucharest in 1984 – and watched a re-run of the Test on television. I hadn't been aware on the night that the team had been presented with their shirts in the changing room by Willie John McBride. The Irish second row had been on five Lions tours as a player, including the two legendary missions of 1971 to New Zealand, and 1974, when he had been captain, to South Africa.

'Here's your shirt, laddie. Now sit down, while I tell you a wee thing or two about what it means to wear this . . .' I just wondered about this ritual. A bit mawkish, perhaps? Did any of the modern players even remember Willie John? Apparently they did, and had been touched by a rare surrender to sentiment by the management.

Perhaps it was just me. I remembered the great man as a not so great manager of the 1983 Lions. Still, the last I had heard of him, before Brisbane, he was running a donkey sanctuary back in Ballymena, which restored him in my book to iconic status.

King O'Malley's was not entirely convinced at first that a re-run of the union Test was a good thing. There were a few customers who wanted to watch the live transmission of State of Origin III. The landlord was an Irishman. Brisbane of the night before was shown in the downstairs lounge before an ever growing number of camp-followers, while the Alfie Langer show, live from Brisbane, was shown in the upstairs bar. It was generally agreed, and this just went to show how easily our opinions could be moulded by our surroundings, that the Irish trio of Rob Henderson, Brian O'Driscoll and Keith Wood had been superb. They were the toast of O'Malley's that night, all right, but even in the cold light of day it would have been true.

That the English formed the bedrock of the team was indisputable. Martin Johnson was a key figure, a brooding, menacing presence to opponents, a tower of strength to his own team. He was the totem. But the other English forwards were not far behind: Danny Grewcock, Phil Vickery, Richard Hill and Martin Corry. It was their mental durability as much as anything. Others had moaned and groaned their way into a state of mutiny, but not these English forwards.

Nor Jason Robinson, Jonny Wilkinson or Matt Perry. However hard the big forwards were, there were also little Englishmen who had opted not for sedition but for the same iron-willed determination to succeed. Austin, of course, was in both camps. Just as he was a midweek rebel, so he was a loyal weekend workhorse.

On this English hard-core, however, others had layered their gifts. This was not England against the Wallabies, but a genuine multicultural force. Tom Smith was the lone Scot, so quiet and so grimly determined that he was more Martin Johnson than Martin Johnson, only a foot shorter. There was a contingent formed by Scott Quinnell, Dafydd James and Rob Howley who had set aside the hysteria that went with being Welsh and a long way from home, and settled instead for calmness and self-belief.

And then there were those Irish. Rob Henderson had thought about giving up smoking on tour, but had decided that this was no time to be putting on weight. He was puffing his way round Australia and hammering the breath out of all who stood in his way. Brian O'Driscoll apparently made coach Andy Robinson tear his hair out. Something along the lines of: who the hell did he think he was? Well, he was the centre who had ripped Australia to bits. And if part of such a player's make-up was a tendency not to give such and such a boring drill with a load of traffic cones and a tackle-bag his total and utter 100 per cent attention, then that was because he was saving it for the real thing. So, tear away, Robbo.

Keith Wood, we noticed in O'Malley's, had done a great deal of kicking in the first Test. And not just the drop-goal attempt. Your man was an incorrigible placer of boot on ball, from scraping it back at the scrums to chips in midfield and lusty hoofs downfield. And yes, the drop goal.

When New Zealand's number eight Zinzan Brook shocked the life out of England with his forty-five-metre drop goal in the semi-final of the 1995 World Cup, he had countered the astonishment by saying that such a moment was what he practised for. It was precisely why he stayed out on the field after the others had gone in to change, and banged over twenty or so field goals. Just in case.

Keith Wood was the same. If you had the skill, you should not be afraid to use it. Before we marked him down as some sort of maverick, however, O'Malley's found itself roaring to every conventional Woody contribution. Like every tackle he made. It was a loud night. The Irish were the green moss covering the bedrock.

A few miles outside Canberra was a peculiar enterprise called Gold Creek Village, in Gunghalin. It was part retail-outlet park and part tourist attraction. Leather-goods franchises sat next to the National Dinosaur Museum, pottery workshops alongside a steam railway. A golf course declared itself 'NOW FULLY OPEN'.

Tucked behind a row of cafés in this strange complex was the Australian Reptile Centre. Well, it was a Monday and didn't seem to be any busier than a Sunday in the capital. So, I found myself paying my few dollars entrance fee and staring into the cold eye of Spot, a diamond python wrapped around a branch by the till.

'Actually, he's not a cold guy at all,' said Ross, who ran the centre. There weren't many customers, and he gave me a personal tour. These were his mates, the frilled lizards, the diamond pythons and the water pythons, and the other snakes who, unlike good old Spot, came armed with a poisonous bite. The brown snake was responsible for most nips, because it was quite at home on farms in the bush. Not even in the bush as such; there were plenty in the countryside around Canberra. Ross was keen to point out, however, that snakes did not like biting people. They did so only if provoked. Alcohol was to blame for the vast majority of cases. Or people wandering around the outback in inappropriate footwear. What was a snake to do in the face of a blundering flip-flop?

The brown snake was only number six in the world's top ten venomous snakes. The tiger snake over there was number four, and over there were the taipans. The central or coastal taipan was number two, and curled up over here was the inland taipan. Number one, top of the hit parade. And sound asleep.

Come on, Ross, how deadly was deadly? Ross paused. This was disloyal. Snakes did not like biting people. They really didn't. Come on, Ross. He sighed and said that before the discovery of snake serum in the mid-1950s, there had only ever been one recorded case of a human surviving a bite by the central or coastal taipan. Wow, and that was only the number two. The venom of Australian snakes worked on the central nervous system, causing the victim's muscles to shut down. You were bitten; you stopped breathing.

Ross checked that his friends were asleep and then told the survivor's story. In 1949 George Rosendale, then eighteen, was working in a carpenter's shop in Queensland. He stepped back and trod on this taipan which was minding its own business, slithering across the floor. The indignant snake struck and sank its fangs through George's boot into the back of his foot. The leather absorbed some of the venom, but George was saved because one of his work-mates rushed up, ripped off the boot and carved out a chunk of George's heel with a chisel.

Ross asked what I was doing in Australia. I said I was over for the Lions. He said he only liked reptiles. Snakes were his mates.

That night the press were invited to a reception at Parliament House. It sometimes happened. Politicians mistook us for people of influence and thought there might be some mileage in us. As far as I knew, no politician had ever sent us a second invitation. The most memorable occasion came in 1990, when England were on tour in Argentina and we were invited to the Pink Palace in Buenos Aires to have breakfast with the President himself, Carlos Menem. And very nice he was, too, and very tasty his mini-croissants. Only the President's secretary did not enjoy our company. She went into Carlos's office to find Chris Jones of the *Evening Standard* filing a few hundred words to his office in London. She thought he had gone in to order a taxi.

We were shown into the foyer of Parliament House in Canberra and waiters appeared bearing trays of drinks and eats. A didgeridoo began to throb on the stairs. Champagne, live music. We were impressed. This might put the Pink Palace to shame. Suddenly the waiters reappeared and began to take the drinks off us. 'Sorry, guys,' we were told. 'This function is for Students of the World.' We looked at each other. Jaundiced eye met jaundiced eye. Students of the World? Easy mistake to make. We were shown upstairs to an annexe at the end of a long cul-de-sac corridor. Our host came to meet us. The Minister for Trade. Oh well.

At least a new set of waiters appeared, bearing copious samples of goods that the trade minister thought would be good for, er, trade. And so earnestly did we co-operate with his export drive that by the time it came to leave I found myself wandering down an even longer corridor and exiting by a side door. A lone security guard waved me on my way. I knew what I was looking for: Commonwealth Avenue, that led from State Circle in a very straight line, over Lake Burley Griffin, back to the city and up Northbourne Avenue. But I found myself blundering through a shrubbery. I really had done my bit for the Hunter Valley vineyards. I somehow remembered what Ross had said about his mate, the brown snake, and where it lived and what caused it to bite. It's funny what sobers you up.

On Tuesday, before the night game at Bruce Stadium against the ACT Brumbies, most of us went to the Australian War Memorial. This was another sobering experience. During the World Cup of 1991 I went to see the Canadians before their quarterfinal match at the Stade du Nord outside Lille in north-eastern France. The Canadians were the forgotten team of that World Cup, having played their pool games deep in the South of France while the rest of the tournament unfurled across the Channel in

Britain and Ireland. But they had beaten Romania and Fiji, and had run France close. They had earned themselves a dip at the reigning Cup holders, the All Blacks, but they felt excluded from the competition's mainstream. They had been shunted from motorway motel to motorway motel, had eaten badly and had been given poor training facilities. Now they were staying in yet another noisy motel in Lille. They were probably going to be soundly beaten by New Zealand.

I met them as they were returning from a visit to the Canadian Memorial on Vimy Ridge. They had been transformed from a bunch of rugby players feeling slightly sorry for themselves into a group of modern Canadians humbled by the knowledge of what their forebears had been through on a sector of the Western Front in the First World War. Gareth Rees, their outside half, was so moved by the visit that he would choose to do his history thesis at Oxford University on the very subject of the assault on Vimy Ridge. The next day, on a rain-sodden rugby field in Flanders, the Canadians were beaten, but their performance was inspired.

After that it seemed to be the norm for teams to pay some sort of homage to their nation's fallen. The All Blacks, a few years later, went to Ypres. The Australian cricketers, before the Ashes series of 2001, visited Gallipoli.

There would be absolutely no point in making such a visit compulsory. There was even a danger that these pilgrimages had become so commonplace that their effect was, if not lost, then diluted. But, as far I could tell, they were still the sort of thing that rugby players would like to do, if only to while away a couple of hours. None of the Lions of 2001 went to the War Memorial in Canberra. They remained locked tight in their rugby prison. Rugby and more rugby.

The supporters and the press streamed in bouncing mood along Anzac Parade, the broad avenue that sweeps from the Parliament building up a slight incline to the Memorial. There were not as many Lions fans here in Canberra as there had been in Brisbane, since most had opted to go north after the Test to Cairns. Reports of Canberra's spookiness had reached their ears.

But this was a special day in this austere city. Up Anzac Parade went this tourist army, full of laughter, and back down they went, two or three hours later, quieter, more solemn. At the base of the lists of names of Australia's fallen in war, 102,000 of them, I met Ivor Taylor, the father of Mark, the Lions centre. Ivor was also a former team-mate and coach of mine at Pontypool. The Taylors were a Blaenavon family, although Mark had moved to, and played for, Swansea. I had just been into the tomb of the Unknown Australian Soldier and around the lists of named dead. I don't know why HMAS *Sydney* should have stuck in my mind, but the roll-call below the ship's name of all hands, 645 sailors, seemed to go and on.

Ivor was emerging from the museums below, where Gallipoli and the First World War dominated one side, the Second World War the other, with a Hall of Valour in between and a new section dedicated to the Anzacs down another flight of stairs. He and I could have sat down in normal circumstances and chewed the fat. But we shook hands in a rather self-conscious fashion and nodded at our surroundings.

'Gets to you, doesn't it?' said Ivor.

I asked him about Mark. 'Well, he was told weeks ago that, however well he played, he wouldn't get a look-in for the Tests. Makes it hard for a lot of players if you tell them that.'

Ivor looked around again. 'There are more serious things for a father to worry about than rugby . . .'

That night the midweek Lions, including Mark Taylor in the centre, the same position Ivor had occupied for Pontypool and Newport, played their last match, against the ACT Brumbies. It was a strange fixture. On paper this should have been one of the highlights of the tour, the Lions taking on the newly crowned champions of the Super 12. The Brumbies, named after the wild horses of the Australian Capital Territory, had become the first team outside New Zealand to take the Super 12 title. And even across the Tasman Sea the title had only ever been won by two teams: the Auckland Blues, who had won it twice under Graham

Henry, and the Canterbury Crusaders, winners for the past three seasons. It was a rare property.

But the fixture had lost some of its glister. Eight of the Brumbies were in the Wallabies squad, and this was merely a midweek game before the second Test. Any Test Lion who was playing was doing so only because of a shortage among the dirt-trackers. Martin Corry, for example, was asked to roll up his sleeves again for a third game in eight days because Colin Charvis was suspended.

Test replacements from Brisbane, on the other hand, were given a run-out. Martyn with a 'y' Williams was chosen along-side Martin with an 'i' Corry in the back row. Iain Balshaw was given yet another chance to try to build some confidence before . . . well, before the tour ended, was the hope for the fullback now. Austin, of course, was also playing. A Lions game would not have been the same without him. This time he was selected on the wing. They were probably fed up with him telling them that he was due a chance there.

In Austin's original tour position, scrum half, Matt Dawson, old Sam Pepys himself, was selected, which made everyone titter. The management had resolutely refused to talk about the Dawson issue since Brisbane. It had been dealt with internally and that was that, insisted Donal Lenihan. Graham Henry was very grouchy on the subject. Matthew had been withdrawn from public display. It was quite good fun to ask the questions about any sanctions just to see the coach's reaction. He reiterated the party line, that the issue had been sorted, Matthew had not been sent home, he had been selected, he'd be taking the kicks at goal, and could we please get on with the Brumbies game?

That game began as if all the undercurrents had converged and finally swamped the midweek camp. Test victory had only further polarised the party. Or the two parties. The Test fifteen had started brilliantly in balmy Brisbane; the dirt-trackers in cold Canberra leaked two tries in the first ten minutes.

The Brumbies were cutting them to pieces. They may have been at least eight short of their full team, but they were winning clean ball up front and behind the scrum were running lines that were completely bamboozling the Lions. This was going to be as painful as the A game in Gosford.

There was a common thread between the two nightmares. Both the Brumbies and Australia A were coached by Eddie Jones. Despite the provocative nature of his comments before his first encounter with the Lions – in fact, it may well have been he who fired the opening salvo in the war of words – there was no doubt that Eddie could coach. He had taken this Brumbies B team to New Zealand to prepare for this encounter with the tourists, and the benefits were now obvious. Short passes were interspersed with long passes; flat, slow running was comple-mented by fast, straight running; quick ball was mixed with slow ball. The Brumbies were throwing variations at the Lions that were beyond the midweek team's defensive skills to stop. Full-back Mark Bartholomeusz went over after six minutes, and left wing Willie Gordon followed five minutes later. The Lions were too confused even to raise much of a protest at a possible forward pass in the first try and a possible knee in touch for the second. Except Austin, who gave referee Peter Marshall hell from start to finish.

Matt Dawson kicked a penalty for the Lions, but it offered only fleeting respite from the assaults on their defence. Even Scott Gibbs looked vulnerable as wing forward Peter Ryan burst through to set up a third try, scored by his back-row partner Des Tuiavii.

The Lions were hardly much better in attack. Matt Dawson missed a penalty and then Scott Murray, the basketball-playing second row with the best hands in the business, dropped a pass from Ronan O'Gara with the line at his mercy. It seemed to sum up the tall Scot's tour.

The Brumbies shrugged off these near-misses against them and began to launch another series of handling movements. At their heart was outside half Pat Howard, who had just returned to Australia following a highly successful period as player-coach with Leicester. So successful, in fact, that he had been voted player of the year in England. With Leicester he had won the Zürich Premiership, the Zürich Championship and, above all, the Heineken European Cup. He had played alongside Dorian West, Martin Corry, Martin Johnson, Neil Back and Austin Healey. And here he was, ripping to bits a side containing three of his former colleagues.

'Take it up!' he shouted, launching that series of moves after the Lions' failed attempts to score. Now, Austin had heard Pat shout this before. It meant Pat was going wide. So, as a good gambler, Austin took advantage of this insider information, and went for the interception.

It worked. The pass from Pat Howard to Mark Bartholomeusz fell only to Austin Healey, who scampered away for the try. Halfway down the pitch he turned and raised a finger, to say thanks to Pat. 'I think he took it OK,' said Austin later.

One who did not take it so well was tall Brumbie second row Justin Harrison. Austin and Justin had previous form together, having had that confrontation during the A game at Gosford. Austin's raised finger re-ignited their personal spat. Justin raced after Austin, and as the winger dabbed the ball down between the sticks and turned to celebrate, the second row barged into him.

'That's just one try, mate,' growled the taller of the two players as Austin, the shorter by at least a foot, bounced off him. 'Otherwise, you're having a hammering.'

The try was but a brief interruption in the one-way traffic. Before the half was over winger Travis Hall kicked another penalty to send ACT in at the interval with a 22–10 lead.

David Young had to do something. His was possibly the most difficult job on tour, trying to keep the mutineers down, to keep up the spirits of the many disappointed players in his care. They had lost in Gosford and now, three days after the epic win by the elite in Brisbane, the discards were staring at an even more emphatic defeat here in Canberra. Did they care? What was the point of even making an effort now? Nobody was going to notice; nobody was suddenly going to say that so-and-so had put his hand up for Test selection. That had been a cruel joke all along, that stuff about seeing who was 'putting up their hand', trying to keep them interested when it was clear the real team had been chosen months before. Why should they bother now?

Dai Young was not one to surrender. In the twilight days of his Lions career he was not about to be accused of letting one of his sides cave in. He asked for one last effort, not for the party as a whole but for the team that was here in the changing room. For the dejected and the rebellious, for themselves.

The second half was one of the emotional highs of the tour. It matched the Brisbane Test for drama. Supporters in Cairns, who had chosen warm weather above cold Canberra, said they burst into tears as the second half unfurled on television sets before them.

Within three minutes of the restart, Ronan O'Gara was upsetting Pat Howard's overall control by obliging him to attend to defensive duties. The out-half of Munster and Ireland was being much more proactive, and within three minutes it was paying off. He dummied and made a break. His fellow Munsterman David Wallace was on his shoulder and went over for the try. Matt Dawson converted; five points separated the teams.

Austin Healey, who had claimed that he might know what made Iain Balshaw click, made good his word. He kicked across the field. Iain had known exactly what Austin was going to do. He ran ahead, caught the kick on the full and was in the clear . . .

'Offside,' said Peter Marshall.

'Bullshit!' said Austin. 'Bullshit, bullshit, bullshit!'

'What did you say?' said the referee.

'I was talking to my team,' said Austin.

'Watch your mouth,' he was warned. As if.

Matt Dawson had two kicks at goal as the increasing tempo of the Lions' game forced the Brumbies to kill the ball. The scrum half missed one and kicked one. The gap was down to two points.

Then came a hitch. Iain Balshaw was chasing his own kick upfield when he floored Mark Bartholomeusz with a high tackle. It was not the most correct tackle of the tour. The Brumbies fullback nearly completed a reverse somersault. Peter Ryan, the ACT wing forward, ran in and slapped the perpetrator. Justin Harrison ran in and swung something more heavy-duty.

Iain was sent to the sin-bin. It might have been the moment

when the comeback by the Lions petered out, but within three minutes Peter Ryan had joined him, guilty of climbing recklessly into a ruck.

Even though the teams were now level on reductions, it seemed that the Lions were feeling their temporary loss more acutely. Ronan O'Gara tried to run out of his twenty-two and was penalised for not releasing the ball. Travis Hall increased the Brumbies' lead to five points. Dawson cut it again with a penalty for offside.

With five minutes remaining on the clock on the giant score-board – and this was the one that counted, rather than the referee's timepiece – the Brumbies very nearly scored a fourth try. In their desperation to prevent it, the Lions conceded a penalty, and the lead was back to five points, at 28–23. The Lions would have to score a try.

They were only penalised again. This time Hall missed the attempt on goal. The Lions, however, were still pinned in their own half. The clock ran down to zero. The hooter sounded. At the next stoppage the referee would blow for full time.

The Lions, however, were in the middle of a move that was unstoppable. It involved just about everyone in the team, but a special mention should be made of the deftness of Darren Morris, the prop, to keep the ball alive as the multi-phased manoeuvre neared the tryline. Out came the ball to Austin. He danced inside and was over. He tried to run round towards the posts, but as Peter Ryan approached, he had to dab the ball down. Ryan still caught him. Normally Austin would have stopped to pass the time of day after such an incident, but he had eyes only for Justin Harrison. He went up to the second row and said, 'That's two tries, pal. And you're about to lose.'

All that remained was for Pepys to write a special entry for himself. The scores were level at 28–all, and Matt Dawson had the conversion to win the game. He said it was the scariest moment of his rugby career. It was about ten metres in from touch. And Matthew took an awfully long time to prepare the tee, the ball, the angle and the distance. And himself.

It never looked like missing. The Lions dirt-trackers mobbed their mutineer-in-chief. This had been their Test, and they had passed it. Matt Dawson was headlines again. Austin said that the conversion persuaded him to cancel the public stoning of the diarist.

Matthew was not invited to the post-match press conference. Tony Roche of the *Sun* was under specific orders to get a line out of the player. It was not as if he had been put in prison, was it? His sports desk needed a quote from Dawson. Not Henry, not Lenihan. Dawson. Tony and a couple of the other journalists tracked Matt down and were having a word with him downstairs. Graham Henry spotted them. Alex Broun arrived with the message that Matt was required upstairs. Matt said that it was OK, he was with a group of blokes he had known a long time. Alex said, 'Now.' Matt shrugged. 'See what it's like, guys?' And off he went.

On the matter of the mutiny and the subsequent clampdown, there was just one more repercussion. And for it we must go back from Tuesday in Canberra to Saturday in Brisbane. Austin had given me a few minutes after the Test, and I had done his *Observer* column. It was always a rush on the Saturday night, because he had to be away on the team bus and I had to do the match report and another piece putting the latest game in its overall context.

I thought I had been pretty careful, given the circumstances of D-Day, Diary Day. Austin paid tribute to the team in general, to the centres in particular and to Martin Johnson. He said that the try by Jason Robinson had not been part of the Test game-plan. But had Graham Henry minded? Not a bit. You should have seen the grin on the coach's face afterwards. And the players hadn't seen too many of those on tour. Austin also talked of the difficulties for the midweek team, now that the Tests were the absolute priority. But who could moan now? Nights like Brisbane made it all worthwhile. That had appeared in the *Observer* the day after the Test. On the Wednesday morning after the ACT game, and while we were still in Canberra, the article was reproduced almost word for word in the *Australian* under the headline, 'Lions Remain Divided: Healey.'

On Wednesday the second Test team was to be announced. I sought out Donal Lenihan to see if he had seen the *Australian*. He said that, unfortunately, Graham Henry had seen the article, thrown the newspaper at Donal and said, 'How much more of this shit do we have to take?'

Donal, bless him, had then taken the whole of the original *Observer* article off the Internet and shown it to the coach. As I was talking to Donal I saw Austin strolling over from the casino to the conference centre where the press conference was being held. And walking towards him was Graham Henry. I ran to intercept them. Too late. Coach met diarist mark 2. It seemed, however, quite an amiable meeting. At the end the coach patted Austin on the shoulder and walked off.

'Did you see that?' said Austin. 'Amazing.' He paused. 'What did you write, anyway?' I began to tell him about Donal and Henry and the Internet, but he held up his hand. 'Don't worry,' he said, 'I don't care.'

Austin had been named as a Test replacement again. I told him that his performance of the night before had been one of the most outstanding individual performances I had seen. He had tackled his heart out, had never given in and had scored two tries. He grinned briefly, but then sat down heavily. He said he thought he might have done enough to win a place on the wing, but was now doubtful for the bench. Justin Harrison had caught him with a knee to his thigh. 'And did you hear what they were calling that referee?' he said. 'They were calling him Marshy this and Marshy that. That's a disgrace.' He limped away, chuffed and uppity in this strange city of Canberra. The Lions had put together two remarkable wins, and as they headed for the second Test in Melbourne they had never seemed less divided.

13

Melbourne, for the second Test

A squad of twenty-seven players was announced for the second Test, which might have constituted an anti-climax had it not triggered a new bout of conspiracy theories. Graham Henry said the delay in giving the final fifteen was caused by a number of bumps and bruises. Plus a few more serious injuries. Matt Perry's groin strain, in particular, was being carefully monitored. Neil Back's ribs were recovering, but they wanted to be sure he would be fully fit to take on George Smith.

So said the coach. What were the real reasons for delaying the team's announcement? Was he playing mind games with the Australians now he had them on the ropes? If Canberra had provided a midweek break complete with its little gem of a game at Bruce Stadium, we were about to re-enter the cauldron of the Test game and all the pre-match sniping that went with it.

Or so we thought. In fact, the tone of the build-up to the second Test on the Wallabies' side was completely different. While we were all still in Canberra they calmly announced their team. There were three changes, two because of injury. Glenn Panoho had hurt a shoulder and was to be replaced at prop by Rod Moore, who had already faced the Lions twice with Australia A and New South Wales. Jeremy Paul's knee injury meant his season was over; Michael Foley of Queensland took over at hooker. Matthew Burke came in for Chris Latham in the only change not determined by injury. The new fullback would

also take the kicks at goal, allowing Andrew Walker to concentrate on the rest of his own wing game.

Graham Henry was asked what he thought of these changes.
He said that Rod Moore, in his two outings against the Lions,
had tended to twist in and under the opposition front row.
Which was illegal. The referee for the second Test, Jonathan
Kaplan of South Africa, needed to be consulted to see what he
would and would not be tolerating at scrum-time. The Wallabies
were playing it straight. Henry was in more probing mood.

This was even before we left Canberra. Now it was time to move
to the Deep South. At the airport I sat down with a group from
Mansfield Rugby Club. They had started out from Nottingham-
shire as a party of twenty-eight, but had split up after the first
Test. One lot had come to Canberra on what they called the
'purists' tour, the other had gone up the Queensland coast to
Hamilton Island, where two of the lads were doing the ultimate
in combining rugby tour with domestic duty. They were getting
married and having their honeymoon on the island. They would
be rejoining the rest of the party in Melbourne.

None of these Mansfield tourists had been to Melbourne
before. It was not on the hit-list of famous rugby union cities.
Melbourne was a sporting Mecca for cricketers, golfers, Grand
Prix motor-racing enthusiasts, horse-racers, tennis fans and,
above all, lovers of Australian Rules football, but it was not
a hotbed of rugby union. For the second time the Wallabies
would be playing on a ground that was not exactly like home.
But if the Gabba had not been used for Test rugby in living
memory, at least it was in a rugby town. Brisbane was home to a
third of the Australian squad. Melbourne was not such an alien
venue that it had never seen a rugby ball before. It had recently
hosted Tests at the Melbourne Cricket Ground. Indeed, the
MCG had briefly held the world record for an official atten-
dance at a rugby Test when Australia played the All Blacks there
in front of 92,000. But it was a risk playing there when the
Wallabies were one down in the series. How many locals would
turn up to watch? The last time a Test had gone to the MCG, for

a Tri Nations game against South Africa, only 38,000 had turned up.

This time the Test was to be played at the brand new Colonial Stadium, just outside the city centre. This was a multi-purpose stadium with a playing surface large enough to accommodate, of course, the game of footie. Aussie Rules stretched over an area the size of a cricket field, with the result that the closing roof at the Colonial was vast in comparison with that of the Millennium Stadium in Cardiff. Cardiff's capacity, at 72,500, was bigger, but the Colonial was more spacious. But would it be full to its capacity of 55,000? Filling the Colonial – and with whom – became the raging theme from the moment we arrived in Melbourne. The stadium was bigger for the moment than the game. The scrummaging technique of Rod Moore was sub-sumed beneath the drive to cram the Colonial. It had never hit maximum before, not even for the most intense of Victorian footie derbies.

But surely, it was pointed out, this game was a sell-out? They'd been saying that at most venues and there had always been the odd empty seat, even at the Gabba. The debate then switched to what colour would predominate on the night of the game. Would it be a repeat of Brisbane, when in the stands Aussie gold turned Lion red? Ten thousand tickets were sud-denly made available, but buyers had to provide an Australian address. The campaign to keep the Lions supporters out had begun. If the Colonial was not going to be ethnically cleansed, then at least it was going to be colour-coded.

And what about the roof? The Lions wanted it to remain open. Rugby, they said, was a test of skills in a variety of conditions, from wind and rain to stillness and sunshine. The forecast suggested wet weather. The Lions came from a wet part of the world. John O'Neil, chief executive of the Australian Rugby Union, said the spectacle came first. If the means existed to guarantee an evening of entertainment then surely they should be used.

The Test coincided with a meeting of the International Rugby Board, the world governing body of the game. Test fever was

rising when the IRB, under their chairman Vernon Pugh, decided
to call a press conference at the Grand Hotel, four hundred yards
from the Colonial Stadium.

The IRB preferred to ponder the big picture at their leisure.
They quite liked, for example, to arrange workshops on the
tackle law. They were currently gently pushing the idea of a
North v South clash of the hemispheres to raise some funds for
global development, although they were fully aware of the extra
demands this would place on players whose welfare and over-
exposure were already very much on their minds. They would
also rather like to provide a vague update of the 2003 World
Cup . . . But details? Well, how about Sweden, Belgium, Switzer-
land and Latvia pre-pre-qualifying from the European Zone for
pre-qualification? Or how about the launch in London six
months henceforth of an awards ceremony for the great and
good of the game, or the relaunch of a rugby yearbook at about
the same time, or announcing the date in November of the latest
Rugby Summit.

No? What sort of details did the press want, then? And why
were there so many of us here that they had had to change
rooms? Normally a dozen turned up to IRB briefings; here there
were a hundred.

The roof? Well, the roof was best left to the two teams
involved. The IRB were sure that an amicable solution could
be reached between the parties. But, um, it would seem that the
views of the host nation might come first. Over to you, John.

John O'Neil was always good for a line. For example, he was
to say later that the Australians had no interest in the North v
South game, since it represented an example of the very player-
overload the IRB were mandated to address. The chief executive
of the ARU had presided over an unprecedented rise in the
profile of rugby union in Australia. And he had not done it the
quiet way. He had slammed England for coming to Australia on
their Tour from Hell with an under-strength party. He had
slammed the planning and the running of the 1999 World Cup.
The IRB liked to mull on the big picture; John liked to get the
bloody painting finished and auctioned off. He said he had

spoken to Syd Millar of the Lions committee about the roof, and amicability had won. The roof would be shut.

If that was a small victory for the Wallabies, they opted for more introverted tactics in the build-up to their enclosed night at the Colonial. After Brisbane they had been given a rough ride in the media. Their preparations had been called into question and their performances on the night had been slammed. They had generally been panned. No individual, with the possible exception of George Gregan, had escaped criticism. The great Michael Lynagh, winner of seventy-two Wallaby caps at centre and outside half between 1984 and 1995, was writing a column on the Internet. He suggested that Stephen Larkham, so patently out of form and injury-prone, should be left out. And he even expressed doubts about the commitment of John Eales. Did the captain have retirement on his mind, rather than the job in hand of beating the Lions? Criticising John Eales was like sticking a sackful of baby koalas in a bucket of water.

The Wallabies responded by going out into the non-rugby city of Melbourne and drumming up support. They put in appearances at the Bourke Street Mall; they spoke at luncheons at the Melbourne Club. And everywhere they went they put their hand up and said, 'Guilty.'

Stephen Larkham said they had been complacent beforehand. He said they had tinkered with their defensive systems too close to the Test. That their tactics on the night had been wrong. That they had worn the wrong studs on the Gabba's surface. That they had let themselves and Australia down. He also made a pledge: it would not happen again. The Wallabies had been ambushed before. They had once conceded over sixty points to the Springboks in Pretoria, even in the reign of Rod Macqueen. They had bounced back then and they would bounce back now. He repeated the pledge: the Wallabies did not play badly twice.

Across town, at the Lions hotel, all was quiet two days before the Test. A sheet of paper was handed out giving the final composition of the team, but neither Graham Henry nor Donal Lenihan was available to answer questions. Matt Perry was fit to play at

fullback. In the back row Neil Back replaced Martin Corry, who
dropped to the bench. Richard Hill moved over to the blind side.
And on the replacements' bench Dorian West came in for
Gordon Bulloch. It was a question of form, was the relayed
message.

Instead of offering coach and manager to the press, the Lions
put forward Steve Black. Blackie was the fitness conditioner on
the tour, a round, jovial Geordie out of whom not a negative
breath could pass. Only good exhalations were permitted,
although it was at times difficult to reconcile the mood of some
of the players with that of the man responsible for their pastoral
care. He oozed the joy of living; they oozed stony-faced fatigue.

Blackie had been one of Graham Henry's first appointments
when the coach arrived in Wales. He was a disciple of uncon-
ventional, even alternative, training methods. He told the players
he loved them and hoped that they could all love each other. In
Henry's second season with Wales the Five Nations formally
welcomed Italy and expanded to Six. Wales performed poorly at
the start of the 2000 Championship and when a few of the
English players were rude about the fitness levels of some of the
Welsh players, a whispering campaign ended in Blackie's resignation and return to the North-East.

Here he was again, reunited with Graham Henry. They made
a strange pair, the ice-cold Kiwi and the roly-poly Geordie, but it
appeared to work for Henry. Blackie seemed to be his sounding
board, his shoulder to cry on, his father confessor. Whether it
worked for the players was another matter. And whether it made
much sense to us two days before the Test was also open to
question.

'I'm obviously – as the fitness conditioner – into the physiol-
ogy of the players,' he told us. 'But I'm into more than that. Their
psychology also. And, if you like, their spirituality. I take the
holistic approach to conditioning.'

Blackie was giving the Lions holistics. The next day the
Australian Rugby Union said it was spending eighty thousand
dollars – about thirty thousand pounds – on give-away mer-
chandise for the supporters at the test: scarves, shirts and hats,

anything that could be painted yellow and green. The colour war was hotting up.

Shortly after the cuddle from Steve Black, I bumped into a small group of Lions players.

How many? That would be telling.

Who? That would be to make life difficult for some of them.

So, were there some Welsh players there, who would be working with Graham Henry after the tour? Yes, but present were representatives of other countries, too. There were no Scots there. That much can be said.

I asked them how they were going. They all rolled their eyes. 'You know how it is,' they said.

They were all midweekers, then? Disgruntled dirt-trackers? Some, granted. But not all. Glancing round, there were one or two from the Test squad . . . but not Austin and not Matt Dawson . . . and, yes, some midweek players.

I said I did indeed know how it was. We had had a lot of fun and games with the diary and the e-mail, the missives from the camp that had been delivered on the day of the first Test in Brisbane. The author of the *Daily Telegraph* diary was all too well known. The e-mail that had arrived on the sports desks of the papers was penned anonymously. I looked at one of the players and said, 'Do you know, your name was mentioned as one of the e-mail suspects? You were in the frame.'

He stared back at me blankly.

'Oh, my God,' I said. 'It *was* you.'

'Maybe,' he said. 'But not just me.'

'Look,' they all said. And they spelt it out for me. And this is a sort of collective summary of what was said: 'There's a great chance that we're going to win this series. And if we do, then there's going to be a lot of credit given to Graham Henry. But it won't be because of him that we'll have won. The players will have done it. And when this is all over and when we get home, we're going to make sure that the world knows exactly how it was done. The players did it their way.'

Did I just make that up? Absolutely not. It happened in the

foyer of the Holiday Inn, the old Central Hotel, on the corner of Flinders Street and Spencer Street.

Well, that was Graham Henry done for, then.

Not necessarily. The coach was a cold fish who spent far too much time for the warmth of his cockles in front of a video screen. But, as Martin Johnson would say, the great revolution in Test rugby, at this rarefied level where detail was everything, was not the slog or the sweat, but analysis. Slog and sweat were as old as the game. Every tour had had its punishment beatings. But analysis was the new key to the lock. Cold analysis.

I didn't know whether Graham Henry had penned the mission statement back in Hampshire, the one about respect and integrity and getting on together. Maybe he had help from corporate script-writers. It just seemed the sort of thing that a headmaster should be able to do pretty well.

But did it mean anything? Perhaps it missed the point by a mile. Why had they made such an attempt at universal harmony? Players whose job depended on their competitive streaks were living on a force-fed diet of rigour. The promise of some fun along the way had long ago been broken. The reality of the tour was that somebody had to grab it and take responsibility for the whole damn thing. And in reality, nothing, but nothing, said that the person who accepted that role of being in charge of an operation as minutely complicated and as unstable as a Test series in Australia had to be popular. Graham Henry might have been held in something less than adoration by his players, by us in the press, but that was the sacrifice he'd made by swapping a cuddly toy for a video-player. The players might be saying they were doing it their way, but Henry still picked the side. He still told them where the Wallabies could be hurt. That was what being a coach was all about. The headmaster knew that it was a lonely job, but that was what being a headmaster was all about. Henry's mission had always been to win the series, not to be mates with his fifth-formers. If the Lions won the series I would still say that Graham Henry deserved all the praise going.

Of course, the series was not yet won. The analysis thus far had been sound. But it would have to be good again. As Henry himself had said, there was a long way to go.

Melbourne was wet and cold. Not exactly wet and cold like Merthyr can be in February, but this was certainly not tropical Townsville. The best way to see this tram-filled city seemed to be to hop on one of the City Circle trams that ran around the perimeter of the central business district. And just follow the advice of the conductor. 'Alight here for Victoria Market. And Melbourne Old Gaol.'

The gaol was cool. Literally so. It was dank and stretched away darkly on three tiers, from the visitors' entrance to the largest display at the far end. This was dedicated to Ned Kelly. Displayed alongside the outlaw's coat of armour and iron helmet with its distinctive eye-slit was the battered Colt 45 he had brandished at his final showdown with the forces of law and order at Glenrowan. Even starker was the scaffold from which he had finally dangled. It was no surprise that the Old Gaol was the only Melbourne museum to make money. The lure of the gruesome.

Nothing could be bleaker than the story of Bob and Jack, the first to be hanged in the gaol. They were a pair of Aborigines who, according to the justice of the times and the fear among polite colonial society that the natives were about to revolt, were intended to serve as a deterrent to others. They were hastily found guilty of murder and even more hastily strung up. Unfortunately, the gallows were not up to the job. Bob and Jack were left twitching on the end of their ropes even as the prison carpenter was finishing off the repairs necessitated by the collapse of the instrument of execution at the first opening of the trapdoor.

Most chilling of all were the artefacts in the cells. On one wall were the printed stories of some of the many murderers hanged here. And on another wall was a case displaying his or her deathmask. To blame was phrenology, the Victorians' attempt to prove that the shape of skulls and features could be linked to criminal behaviour. I began to feel my way round the back of my skull. I could be as phrenologically-minded as the next man. And I was musing that these mementoes of spine-tingling science proved only one thing: that people were very small in those days. But that it all served to make you think twice about where you sprinkled your cyanide. I was pondering this when a voice outside the cell murmured, 'Pontypool boys should be at home in here, Edwoot.' And the heavy wooden door closed behind me, leaving me alone with my small-faced cell-mates.

That afternoon Graham Henry gave his own theory of skulls. The second Test was all about 'the top three inches', he stated. Brainpower would determine who would win and lose the game. The Lions wanted to finish the series off here in Melbourne. A decider in Sydney would be 'a lottery'. They had spent the week coming to terms with the role-reversal since Brisbane and their transformation from underdogs into favourites.

The following day was damp in Melbourne. Not that it mattered a jot now that the roof at Colonial Stadium was going to be closed. Fly-sheets were being distributed across the city imploring the Wallabies fans to wear yellow and gold. Out on the streets it seemed a waste of paper. From mid-morning the Lions supporters were out in force, bedecked in red. The morning was dedicated to strolling in front of the bars and restaurants on the South Bank, the redeveloped docklands of the Yarra River. And having worked up a bit of a thirst, the afternoon was reserved for sitting down and pouring ale down their throats and millions of Australian dollars into the local economy. Once again the fans were exemplary in their conduct, even if their version of 'Waltzing O'Driscoll' did not seem to be catching on among the odd small gang of yellow-and-gold jumpers that passed by. The Colonial Stadium, four hundred yards away, awaited their arrival.

By 6.30 that evening the atmosphere at the ground was echo-electric. A resonating pulse of sound went up and back down off the closed roof and then around the vast enclosure. The Australians had merely been timing their arrival with care. The stadium that had never been filled before was bursting to capacity with a record crowd of 56, 605. The Lions supporters were at last outnumbered. Yellow and gold shimmered from the ground all the way up to the ceiling.

'You're only wearing yellow 'cos it's free,' retorted the red choirs.

Austin was not fit to take his place on the bench. The Test for him was not about his top three inches but an area of bruising about two feet off the ground. The blow to his leg from Justin Harrison in the Brumbies game prevented him from running freely. Neil Jenkins was called up to sit among the seven replacements.

On the opposing side there were no late hiccups. The only late change here was the volume of noise behind the Wallabies. Australia, at last – and in this non-rugby city – was discovering what it was like to align its support, body and soul, behind the posh old game of union. Daniel Herbert, the robust, uncompromising heart of the midfield, walked out first in recognition of the fiftieth Test appearance he was making tonight. He emerged into a wall of noise. The name of John Eales caused the roof to rise another couple of centimetres as it was announced that he was captaining his country for the fiftieth time.

Would the support last? The Australians had promised not to play badly again. They won the first line-out on the Lions' throw. They watched as Matt Perry kicked directly into touch from outside his own twenty-two. But for their own first line-out, Michael Foley, the stand-in for the injured Jeremy Paul, tried a trick throw. It did not come off. Matt Burke kicked straight into touch. It was a twitchy start by both teams.

In the third minute came the first break. Martin Johnson claimed an orthodox line-out and Dafydd James came off his right wing and cut straight through midfield. Perhaps the support remained a touch distant, perhaps the Welsh winger saw his chance to beat Matt Burke one-to-one. Whichever; he held on to the ball and the moment was lost.

It did not seem to matter. The momentum had been established. Within two minutes, Martin Johnson was winning another line-out and the Wallabies were straying offside. Jonny Wilkinson kicked the penalty.

Five minutes later the gap opened out to six points. Toutai Kefu, the Wallabies number eight, climbed into a ruck, pumping his knees and stamping on Lions' limbs. Referees would tolerate a certain amount of 'clearing' of opponents' bodies, but once the action became too much of a can-can, they were likely to intervene. Jonathan Kaplan of South Africa did just that, and Wilkinson completed the admonition by adding his second penalty.

It was all going bruisingly smoothly for the Lions. Matt Burke missed a kick at goal after Tom Smith dived over the ball at a ruck. Any tension seemed to be one-sided now.

But then came the first twist. The Lions began to find themselves under extreme pressure in their own twenty-two. Rob Howley fed Jonny Wilkinson after a kick by Stephen Larkham had sent both halfbacks scurrying back towards their own line. Wilkinson was clattered but the Wallabies were penalised for their eagerness to rip the ball and several bodily bits off the Lions' central character.

Jason Robinson then fed infield to Matt Perry in the Lions' twenty-two. Again the player was overwhelmed, only for the tacklers to see the scrum feed given to the defenders. At last, though, the pressure told. Scott Quinnell picked up and drove from the defensive zone and was penalised for not releasing. Matt Burke kicked the penalty, and the gap was down to three points.

Then came the second twist. If the tide had threatened to turn once, now it looked like turning again the other way. The Lions wrested control with a massive series of tackles, but not before they had once again unveiled the delights of Brian O'Driscoll. The Irish centre cut through as he had done in the first Test. Perhaps with even more grace. Now all he had to do was finish off the sublime moment. He had Matt Perry outside him. He chose to go it alone as he had done in the first Test. And this time he was tackled.

Again, it seemed not to matter. Scott Quinnell smashed

Stephen Larkham in a tackle. Danny Grewcock made a double tackle even as he was falling over. Richard Hill collared Andrew Walker and stopped him dead. O'Driscoll leapt, hands up, for a high ball against George Gregan and beat the scrum half hands down. Hill chased a cross-field kick by Wilkinson and was only denied a try by Andrew Walker taking the ball into touch.

So many mini-triumphs for the Lions. But they had to generate points. In the midst of the specks of success came a try. From the line-out set up by Hill's challenge on Walker, Grewcock won possession and the Lions set up one of the forward drives that had always been assumed to be their principal weapon in the series. That they had not featured large yet, and that the Tests were a riot of running, seemed irrelevant now as the Lions swarmed around the ball, isolated it and drove. There could only be one scorer here. Neil Back steered these mauls for Leicester and England like an advanced driving instructor. He now did it for the Lions, manoeuvring the swaying and bucking beast of a vehicle to, and over, the tryline.

The series was there for the taking. The Lions were in control. They led by eight points, and there were still some of those mini-triumphs to come. Jonny Wilkinson tossed Matt Burke into the air. Scott Quinnell charged through an attempted tackle by the fullback.

But something went wrong. Perhaps it was started by Owen Finegan's tackle on Matt Perry, which showed that muscularity was not all one-way. Perhaps it was the pair of turnovers the Lions conceded as the first half ended.

Perhaps. But it was more likely to be the loss of the best forward on tour. Richard Hill was already bleeding from the nose when he was caught off the ball by a trailing arm belonging to Nathan Grey. In the light of all the accusations by Bob Dwyer and Eddie Jones about how busy the Lions could be off the ball, this seemed a little rich, and would certainly become one of the points for discussion in the days ahead. But it was never quite clear whether the centre hit the wing forward with his elbow – which would have been truly reprehensible, if not life-threatening – or with a bit of upper arm betwixt shoulder and elbow.

It looked bad, and it certainly was as far as Richard Hill was concerned, for he was pole-axed by the blow. His tour was over. The Lions had lost their invisible giant. But whether it was as premeditated as some of the more hysterical reactions would have had us believe would remain just one of those rugby mysteries. Debates on half-seen moments would keep us arguing for as long as the human eye and the television camera failed to register the details of split-second incidents.

The Lions were hardly keeping their own nobbly bits to themselves. Scott Quinnell had already floored Stephen Larkham with a shoulder-charge after the fly half had kicked the ball. Rob Henderson was about to make a similar challenge. The shoulder-charges of the Lions and the elbow-arm of a Wallaby were to become a morality play in their own right, but for the moment there were only immediate consequences. Hill left the field, came back, but soon it was clear he was suffering from concussion. He departed for good. Larkham had lengthy treatment and was left dangling his right arm by his side. But he stayed on the field.

The high tackles on the Wallaby play-maker were penalised. Matt Burke reduced the gap with his second penalty. At half-time the Lions led 11–6.

Martin Corry replaced Richard Hill in the second half. It would be terribly unfair to pin any blame for what was to come on the substitute back-row forward, who had quickly become one of the characters of the tour. Martin offered a raft of skills, from ball-catching at the line-out to ball-carrying in the loose. He was also one of the uncomplaining workhorses of the party who was cramming in game after game without a break.

But he wasn't Richard Hill. In the second half, George Gregan, who had been one of the few Wallabies to escape criticism after Brisbane, began to run the show. He'd been effective in adversity, and now he found himself living in affluence. Life without Richard Hill in his face was a lot easier. And life with a ten-point lead was even sweeter.

The Lions' five-point advantage vanished in all the time it took for Joe Roff to run in two tries at the start of the second half. And this was how it happened: Jonny Wilkinson made a mistake. That is not a sentence that will be written often in the history of rugby. Jonny was on his own twenty-two when he tried to float a pass to the right wing. Joe Roff intercepted, and away he went. Brian O'Driscoll ran back and made enough of an effort to force the left wing into touch at the corner for the referee to call for the video replay. The Wallabies were sure immediately that they had scored. The video-ref soon confirmed their impression.

The scores were level. And within seconds Australia were in the lead, as the Lions strayed offside and Matt Burke kicked a penalty. Two minutes later a Lions scrum was wheeled and driven on its own put-in. Jonny Wilkinson was not to blame for this. The forwards lost collective concentration for a moment, were caught off-balance and lost one against the head.

The scrum broke up. John Eales, of all people, picked up the ball from his second-row position and ran away with it. He fed George Gregan who fed Stephen Larkham who sent Joe Roff on his way again. The wing had more to do this time, but soon Dafydd James was left behind and Jason Robinson, covering from the other wing, was left spinning as Roff cut inside.

It was as devastating a burst as the Lions' spree that decided the first Test. The game was over even before the second half was ten minutes old.

Or was it? The Lions were awarded penalties, one against prop Nick Stiles for stamping, another for a less brutal offence at a ruck. Jonny Wilkinson kicked only one, but it meant the Lions now trailed by the margin of just one converted try. There was hope yet.

All the defining incidents, however, were to be regulated by the home side. When, for example, Brian O'Driscoll cut back infield to make what might have turned into another genius-play, Nathan Grey cut him in two with the tackle of the game.

And then Australia sealed their win with the try of the match. From a line-out they swept from one side of the field to the other in a series of charges and rucks from which the ball was instantly recycled. George Gregan spat little passes to forwards on the charge against a defence going backwards. Owen Finegan, slated after his first-Test performance, was the last forward involved, charging and then floating a pass out of the tackle to Matt Burke who crashed between Iain Balshaw and Jason Robinson for the try. Finegan's reputation was restored. Meanwhile, two of the best attacking runners in the European game, one leggy and long-striding and totally out of touch, the other tight-muscled and darting and exhilaratingly successful, met in a tangle underneath a Wallaby try-scorer.

They weren't the only players to end up in a heap. Seven minutes after the try the Lions conceded a penalty. Martin Johnson did not release after a tackle. But eyes were not focused on the guilty captain, but on a smaller player lying on the ground nearby. Physios and doctors ran on to attend to Jonny Wilkinson. They called for a stretcher. The outside half was carried from the playing arena. As an added insult, the penalty was kicked.

Two more by the same Matt Burke and the fullback who had been left out of the starting line-up in Brisbane had returned a personal tally of twenty-five points. The Wallabies had rattled up a record team tally against the Lions: thirty-five. They had said they would not play badly twice, and they had kept their word. The Lions had been crushed in the second half.

But how different it might have been. Up at half-time, the Lions had needed only a period of consolidation at the start of the second half. Instead, they had been ambushed. The insurrectionists of Brisbane had been bushwhacked in Melbourne.

Disappointment among the following faithful was tempered by the knowledge that the series would be decided in Sydney, at Stadium Australia in the Olympic Park. A grand showdown would surely be no bad thing.

The Wallabies began to think immediately of the game ahead. Rod Macqueen at the press conference after the victory announced that he was bringing forward his retirement, from the end of the Tri Nations to the end of this Lions series. He had eight days left in the job. He said he wanted the decision, which had been preying on his mind for some time, out of the way, so that the Wallaby camp might concentrate solely on the decider ahead.

The Wallabies had made a second pledge with regard to the Lions series. They had said that they would be at their best in Sydney. Could the Lions, who were in a state of shock in their changing room, shaking their heads in disbelief at what had just befallen them, say the same about themselves? They knew a great chance had slipped through their fingers. Donal Lenihan could do no more than look down at his little notebook and read out a long list of injured. Jonny Wilkinson was in hospital with a feared broken leg. Brian O'Driscoll, Rob Howley and Richard Hill were also there with injuries to neck, ribs and jaw respectively. Even with the best that holistics could offer, the Lions' task was now Herculean.

14

Sydney Part 2: Test 3

There was to be no midweek game before the third Test. This would allow the coaches to concentrate on the main event. But since they had long ago abandoned the Tuesday players, leaving them to their own, brief preparations on a Monday, it now meant that there was a team-load of players wandering around with nothing to do. The dirt-trackers had reached their pinnacle in Canberra with that comeback against the Brumbies. They were demob happy now, while the Test team were obviously dejected.

Back to Manly the party trudged from Melbourne. At least it was a return visit to the beachside hotel, with training facilities just around the corner at the Oval and with easy access to Sydney itself by ferry across the harbour. Despite the defeat in Gosford and the night of the brawl against the Waratahs, everybody had enjoyed – and it was a relative term on the HMS *Bounty* – round one of the stay in sunny Manly.

Now it was raining, and the Tasman Sea was sludge-grey outside the hotel windows as the Lions limped back.

On Monday Keith Wood went solo at the daily press conference.

'Woody, what are you doing here?' the Irish hooker was asked.

'Well, I suppose I was the only one stupid enough to say I'd do it,' he replied.

'Woody, after what's just happened to you in Melbourne,' came the next question from the floor, 'have you now got to contemplate . . . defeat in the decider?'

'Jayz, lads,' said Keith. 'I thought you were going to say "contemplate suicide". It's not that bad, I can assure you.'

He talked of the need to rebuild spirits. Nothing too rushed. Let Saturday's defeat sink in and let the thoughts of Sydney begin to brew naturally. Nothing could be rushed. Bruises to mind and body needed time.

That afternoon Keith and Martin Johnson, Austin Healey and Iain Balshaw could be seen messing about on the beach. They were positively frolicking. Passers-by had to do a double-take to see if these really were Lions players enjoying themselves.

Some bodies were bruised beyond repair in time for the Test. That night Robert Howley and Richard Hill sat in a corner and watched the Wimbledon men's final through the heads and shoulders of a large crowd in the hotel bar. Robert's ribs were broken and Richard was suffering from concussion after the collision with the controversial part of Nathan Grey. There was no point in asking Richard about it. 'Can't remember a thing,' he said.

For some strange reason there seemed to be a fair amount of support for Goran Ivanisevic in the tennis. Pat Rafter had the Manly locals on his side, but those from the outside were backing the wild-card underdog. Croatia was adopted for the night. Not surprisingly, even tennis support brought with it the nationalistic tensions of the Balkans. A row broke out between a couple of locals and a pair of Lions supporters. Punches with the power of a backhand drop-volley swung and missed. 'Best fun we've had on tour,' said the two RH's, Howley and Hill, from their corner seats.

On Tuesday it rained and rained. I went to the Manly Aquarium, because I obviously needed some more water.

Ross from the Reptile Centre in Canberra had told me that there were only two predators in Australia, the shark and the saltwater crocodile. That was all very reassuring, but there seemed to be an inordinate number of creatures in this land that could pack a fearful defensive punch. And we weren't talking television tennis tantrums. Stonefish, pufferfish, blue octopus, box jellyfish, lion fish. It was not wise to stand on them, eat them, touch them or even approach them to tell them they had beautiful eyes. And that was just in the water. The redback spider and funnel-web spider had the upstairs of the aquarium to themselves, along with a few of Ross's snakes. And a scorpion or two. Australia packed a mean retaliatory clout.

That afternoon I went into the sea for a dip. Getting wet was by now an obsession. There were Lions in the water, Darren Morris and Jeremy Davidson, belly-boarding in the waves. I was being so careful not to step on anything noxious that I did not notice that the breakers were rather aggressive. I was picked up by one and thrown back into the shallows in a cartwheel of arms and legs. The Lions did not hang around long either.

I went to the Tuesday press conference that replaced the Tuesday game, with salt water leaking from every orifice. Phil Larder, the defence coach, was up on stage. He talked about how it had been a rush to modify and improve the defensive structures he had built with England. He said he was happy with the way the Lions had adapted to his systems. It was easy to be mesmerised by Phil's training patterns, but the principles were relatively simple. I think. The defensive line had to keep its shape, straight and tightly manned, concentrated, compressed even around the breakdown without being necessarily committed to it. It was designed to stretch outwards, towards the touchlines, to deal with an apparent overlap. What really caused trouble was penetration at a weak spot in the middle of the chain. Slower forwards should be kept closer to the breakdown, to use their bulk tackling the oncoming hard-yard busters. Advancing into the tackle was all-important. And technique: stay low and drive upwards.

There was not much, Phil said, the defence could have done about the two Joe Roff tries in Melbourne – the interception and the scrum-steal – that had set the Wallabies on their way. After that, the Lions were chasing the game and mistakes were bound to happen. He then spent quite a time on the question of the blow to Richard Hill and the tackles on Stephen Larkham. In his book, and this was one written over many years in rugby league, any tackle involving the elbow and occurring off the ball was suspect, possibly to the point of being criminal. He was surprised that the citing commissioner had not taken action against Nathan Grey. Richard Hill, the victim, would be missing the Test. The perpetrator should be similarly absent. As for Larkham, he had been hit by players committed to the tackle, who were leading with their shoulder, not their elbow. The law actually stated that arms had to be used in the tackle. But this, I thought to myself, was apparently not a point of law, but of justice beyond the whistle. Players, even in split-second readjustments to accommodate a change of angle or a shift of balance, knew what they were doing. They knew what would happen if they left an elbow up or dropped a shoulder. In the armless armoury of the limb used as a lethal weapon, the shoulder fell within the Geneva Convention, while the elbow was proscribed.

I was musing on all this and thinking that it was bound to work the Australian papers into a tizz – it didn't – when Dr James Robson came into the press conference. The arm was not the only limb in question. This was also the week of the leg: of Jonny Wilkinson's shin and Lawrence Dallaglio's knee.

Should Lawrence have come on tour? His employers at Wasps obviously thought not. Their star player had hurt his knee in a club game, and if he had stayed at home he would have mended in time for the new season. Instead, he went on tour with the Lions, broke down again in the Waratahs game, needed reconstructive surgery and now faced being out of rugby possibly for a whole year. Not surprisingly, Wasps, with a salary to pay for zero productivity, were not exactly thrilled. A story briefly did the rounds that the London club were thinking of sueing the Lions.

For the moment, however, James had better news to report. Jonny Wilkinson had not broken his leg. There was only soft-tissue damage to his lower leg. This was Tuesday; the medical team were engaged in a race to have the fly half fit for Saturday.

To all onlookers it had seemed impossible to contemplate Jonny's inclusion in the Sydney team as he was taken by stretcher from the field in Melbourne. James Robson confirmed that Jonny had not been able to look down at his leg. It had gone completely numb, and he was convinced that it was broken. But now there was a fifty–fifty chance that he would be ready in time.

James's was one of the most difficult jobs in the game. He was always in the position of having to make judgements on injuries in the face of pressure from coaches – and the injured players themselves – to declare them sufficiently healed to allow participation in a full-contact sport. If it went wrong you might have a player out for a year. If you practised your science and your art well, you might almost miraculously have a player off a stretcher and back in the Test arena within a week.

James sat there talking about the need to cut down the number of games in a season, of swimming-pool therapy and intensive physiotherapy. Of rest and respect for the body. Phil Larder was there talking about aggressive defence, of shoulders and elbows. They made a strange pair.

After the press conference I bumped into Austin in the foyer. He asked what I had written after the Melbourne Test. It had been a bit tricky to contact him immediately after the game, given the result and the lack of a mobile phone signal in the basement of Colonial Stadium. In the end he had jumped off the team bus and we had grabbed a couple of minutes by the exhaust pipe.

At 1.30 on Sunday morning, while I was finishing off the match report, having sent Austin's column a couple of hours earlier, Alex Broun phoned to ask if I was going to file anything by Austin. I said I was. He asked me, in the light of the Matt Dawson diary and the Healey quote-backs on divisions in the camp, to let him see a copy. I said I was right up against the deadline in London and that I wouldn't have time. He asked me to read it to him. I did, skipping over a few Austinisms to make it even blander than it already was.

I told Austin it was fine. Innocent tosh about the boys being gutted, the chance lost, his own injury, about the difficulties of raising spirits again. But it could be done. The Lions weren't finished yet. Stuff like that.

On Wednesday the Lions announced their team for the Sydney Test. The one that would decide the series. There was one enforced change in the back row. Martin Corry came back on the blind side for Richard Hill. Then, lo and behold, Austin appeared in the starting line-up, on the wing instead of Dafydd James. In fact it was a right rebels' outing. Matt Dawson was at scrum half instead of Rob Howley.

There was good news on the very non-rebellious Jonny Wilkinson. He was announced in the team. His chances of playing had gone up to 70–30. If ever one name acted as a mood swingomctcr, it was Jonny's. Or, two names. Brian O'Driscoll was also declared fit to play. Given the list that Donal had rcad out in Melbourne, the injury bulletin was about as good as could be.

I thought it would be more appropriate to see Austin now. At the other Test-team announcements the players had been made available on the spot, and we were told that no contact could be guaranteed after that. Players began to appear. In came Colin Charvis and Martyn Williams, who were both on the bench, as they had bccn in Brisbane. Colin was asked how it felt to be back there. He said he had been on the bench before. It was no big deal. He was asked if he was looking forward to the Test. He said he was looking forward to going home. Then, with an audible sigh, the big wing forward made an effort to sound enthusiastic. 'We'll make one final effort. Dig deep for one last blast. And then we can go home.' Effort, effort. It was all a bit of an effort.

Now, I had every sympathy with Test replacements, but I needed to see the full-on number fourteen. Austin had gone from being number three scrum half to number two outside half, and was now number one right wing. It might make the easiest column of the tour.

He was nowhere to be found. Nobody could trace Matt

Dawson either. The two most newsworthy players of the hour were being kept away. Suddenly, Austin was spotted leaving the hotel. He was intercepted and brought upstairs to the mezzanine area where a crowd quickly gathered around him. He was asked how he was going to stop Joe Roff, given that they had met before and Joe had, well, gone round Austin a couple of times. The Lions' new right wing said the only thing that wasn't knackered on him was his tongue. Perhaps he could talk Joe to a standstill.

When he had finished he came over to me by the lifts. He wasn't moving very well. The leg still, I asked? No, just a bit stiff, he replied. Come on then, I said, let rip. You're in the team.

No. Austin was in mellow mood. He paid tribute to Dafyyd James, who hadn't done anything wrong. He said that obviously he was pleased to be in the team at last. He reckoned he might have had a shout at being selected for the second Test if it had not been for his injury. So, he was pleased with everything, but he was still pretty fed up with the tour . . .

And here he noticed a couple of Australian journalists who had edged closer as we were talking. They were taking notes. I asked them to give us a bit of space. I think I may have hit them with a bit of pomposity: 'This is Austin's personal column, you know.'

'That's what really pisses me off,' said Austin. 'The way they're always taking half-bits of other people's words and firing them back at you. What is it with this place?' And he then launched into a rant against Australia. Not all of it; just the human male inhabitants. 'They can't help rubbing our noses in it. All the time.' He said he had never cheered so loudly for anyone as he had for Goran Ivanisevic in the Wimbledon final.

He eventually turned to go. He really was not moving well. 'You know Justin Harrison's been selected for the Wallabies?' I asked. Justin was indeed in for the injured David Giffin. Austin nodded. 'Might be good to keep your duel brewing.'

'If you like.' And off he went.

There was no need to write up the Austin column until Thursday, for publication on Friday morning in the *Guardian*. And there was no real rush to write it up first thing on Thursday either. I killed some time by talking with Dave Alred, the Lions' kicking coach, about the Summit ball they used in Australia. He said it wasn't very good. Not very good at all. Adidas, for example, had been down the same technological and design route as Summit years previously, and had been quick to move on and embrace more advanced science.

Dave knew his kicking. He'd kicked in league and he'd kicked in union and he'd even kicked in American Football with the Minnesota Vikings. He could punt the ball into orbit, he could drop goals from Perth to Adelaide and he could place-kick the distance of Neil Jenkins and Jonny Wilkinson combined. If he said the Summit ball wasn't very good, then that was fine by me.

Of course, a kicking coach had a duty to stand by his kickers if their strike rate wasn't quite as impeccable as usual. The Tests had seen explosions of running rugby, which probably wasn't what turned Dave on, just as conceded tries tended to set Phil Larder's teeth on edge. 13–0 to the Lions, thanks to no missed attempts, a drop goal from sixty metres, a penalty from halfway plus the conversion of a try conceived as a result of research-analysis into the only possible way to break down the Wallabies' defence, would have had them drooling.

It was all quite relaxed. The mood had gone from gloomy to evenly balanced. We wandered up to Manly Rugby Club on the edge of the Oval behind the hotel for a press conference given by Andy Robinson. He said absolutely nothing at all. Or rather, he gave away absolutely nothing at all. 'Did I say anything?' he asked Chris Hewett of the *Independent* afterwards. 'Nope,' said Chris. 'Excellent,' said Andy.

I wrote up Austin that afternoon. The Aussie male took a bit of stick for rubbing the Poms' noses in it the whole time. Australian women and children were fine, but not the blokes. Goran had received Austin's support at the tennis. And wasn't it strange that both Austin and Justin Harrison were selected for the final

Test? Their personal feud was bound to come to a head just as the whole series was to be decided at Stadium Australia.

Austin had told me that if opposition players were so wound up by what he said that they came gunning for him, then they would not play rugby very well. In went a 'plod' and a 'plank' for Justin from their first encounter in Gosford; an 'ape' from Canberra. That would do nicely, I thought, and headed off across Sydney Harbour by water taxi to dinner at Doyle's on the Beach at Watsons Bay.

In the newspapers the next morning there was a brief story about Keith Murdoch, the former New Zealand prop who had been living in outback Australia more or less ever since he was sent home in disgrace from the All Blacks' tour to Britain and Ireland in 1972. All in the one day of 2 December of that year, Murdoch managed to score a try in the first-Test win over Wales, fall out with his tour manager Ernie Todd and punch out the lights of Peter Grant, a security guard at the Angel Hotel in Cardiff. The prop was expelled from the tour, but instead of going home to New Zealand, he took a detour from Singapore to Australia, where he had been living, working and staying out of the limelight ever since. Occasionally he strayed back into the news. In 1979 on a rare return visit to New Zealand he had given mouth-to-mouth resuscitation to a drowning toddler. Then, after the New Zealand rugby writer Terry McLean tracked him down to a remote pub in Western Australia, Murdoch told him to leave before he had his face shoved in a puddle of oil.

Murdoch was now required as a formal witness at the inquest into the death of Kumanjai Limerick, a twenty-year-old Aborigine who had been found dead in a crater at an old goldmine called Nobles Nob, near Tennant Creek in Northern Territory. Tennant Creek was an isolated town of four thousand inhabitants on the road that stretched a thousand miles between Alice Springs and Darwin. Limerick had been well known as a petty thief who would break into houses for some grog. He had broken into Keith Murdoch's house the previous October, and not long afterwards had been found dead. Murdoch had disappeared again, although, according to the newspaper story, he had just been found. The paper printed the transcript of a conversation one of its reporters had tried to have with the former All Black. It was clear that when a New Zealander decided to keep his mouth shut, not much would ever escape.

That afternoon at the Manly Rugby Club I tried to find out how Graham Henry was coping with the build-up to the big occasion. I had spoken to him way back at Tylney Hall in sunny Hampshire in England, but in Australia he had decided to do no one-on-one interviews. He did his press conferences, sometimes offering a neat one-liner, but then glided away. Sometimes he could be seen strolling down to the beach with Nick Bishop, who would be writing his tour book.

It was the most amazing tour. Everybody was writing a column for a newspaper, doing a book, appearing in television documentaries, keeping written diaries or radio diaries, or writing on the Internet either anonymously or with a byline. Everybody but everybody was being asked to write something on the tour. And everybody had been told not to reveal anything.

Talking of not revealing anything, Martin Johnson was asked first how he was dealing with the pressure. The captain said that he could not afford to become too stressed because he had to play, and if you were too agitated you would not be able to perform. But the very act of playing was at least a release.

I asked the coach how he was coping, given that he did not have the same release of physical exertion as the captain.

'What do you mean?' he replied.

'Well,' I said, 'It's well known that you don't sleep very well, that you can be found watching videos at four in the morning . . .' What did I mean? 'Well, how are you sleeping?'

'Fine,' he said. 'I slept with my wife last night. All night, thank you.' The room chuckled.

For the rest of the briefing he went through the usual stuff about the size of the challenge, how Jonny Wilkinson was now 90 per cent fit and by the next day would be 100 per cent. Games such as these were what you went into coaching for. A thespian could probably do wonders with the words of Graham Henry, but the coach's own clipped Kiwi delivery announced, as it always did: 'The shutters are up and you aren't coming in.'

As I was heading back to the hotel I caught up with the coach, who was waiting for some traffic lights to change.

'Why did you ask me that question?' he said.

'Because something very special might happen tomorrow,' I replied. 'Something epic in sporting terms. But without any human detail, it will lack . . . romance.' As we stood there, waiting for the little green man to start flashing, I did hesitate on the word 'romance'.

'You're right,' said Graham Henry. I nearly stepped out in front of a bus. 'If you must know, I woke at two in the morning and couldn't get back to sleep. I read until about four and then dropped off. Wide awake again at 5.45. Raewyn was there, but there's not a lot she can do to help. She's used to it.'

We began to cross the street. 'It's simple now, isn't it?' he continued. 'After all the . . . all the complexities of the tour, it's come down to this. The formula is this simple: if the Lions play well tomorrow, we'll win the series. If the Wallabies play well and we play well, we'll win.'

We arrived at the hotel. Waiting in the foyer was Ian McGeechan, the coach of the Lions tours of 1989, 1993 and 1997. With his lopsided grin on, Graham went over to greet him. The sludge-grey skies had lifted. Manly was bathed all over in deep blue.

The next morning I was leaving the hotel to enjoy the early-morning sunshine of Test day, when I bumped into Austin. He was on the pavement with James Robson. Doctor and player were reading the newspaper.

'It's come back at us again,' said Austin. He didn't look best pleased. 'I read what you'd written on the Internet. I thought some of it was a bit close to the mark.' He turned stiffly and walked away. He'd just failed a fitness test. He was out of the Test. The doctor and he had just returned from hospital where a scan had revealed a bulging disc. They had been to a chiro-practor's, where manipulation and a 'click' had helped to an extent, but not sufficiently to make it possible for Austin to take his place on the grand stage. All I could think was that I had promised Austin I'd make his mother put away her firearm. Another broken vow.

The loss of Austin created more problems than the simple necessity to replace him on the wing. That bit was easy. Dafydd James returned to the position he had occupied in the first two Tests. He had hardly put a foot wrong, so there was no sense of panic there. But Austin had also provided cover for scrum half. If anything happened to Matt Dawson, there was now nobody to replace him. Rob Howley and his ribs were confined to sitting in the corner drinking beer with Richard Hill and not laughing.

At Melbourne Airport I had bumped into Rupert Moon, the scrum half of Llanelli and formerly of Wales, who was on tour with a bunch of friends from his old home-town club, Walsall. You knew they were in town because wherever they stayed they hoisted a giant banner: 'Walsall RFC. Wim ere yew ay.' Which apparently translated as, 'We're here, you're not.' Which, itself, needed a translation.

Rupert was bouncing through Melbourne in his inimitable style. Well, perhaps not inimitable: Tigger in *Winnie the Pooh* was very similar. I asked him, as you do, whether he had brought his boots with him.

'Of course,' he replied, stopping for a fraction of a second. 'You think,' bounce, bounce, 'I'm joking, don't you?' Bounce.

In the end it wasn't the Tigger of Llanelli who became a Lion, but Andy Nicol of Glasgow Caledonians and Scotland. He must have thought Donal Lenihan was joking when the manager rudely interrupted his gentle tour around Australia in charge of a group of supporters with a call to the Lions' replacement bench. Of course he didn't turn down the offer. In fact, as long ago as 1993 he had been taking late calls from the Lions and turning up as a replacement.

As I was setting out for the stadium I bumped into Andy, who was going down in the hotel lift. He was leafing through a thick pile of notes. The line-out calls, the moves, the patterns, the annotated paraphernalia of six weeks' work . . . 'I thought I'd done with revising for exams,' he said.

I went to the game by ferry and train, rather than media bus. The Manly ferry was one of the highlights of the stay in Sydney. As the boat churned across the harbour from the wharf in Manly Cove to Circular Quay in the heart of the city, rounding the various promontories on the way, the Sydney skyline was slowly peeled back. On this day the sights were even more striking than usual, as the ferry itself was awash in red and speckled with yellow and green.

I went up to the seating area in the bow and asked a man wearing a Wallaby shirt if the seat next to him was free. 'No, mate. That's taken,' he said gruffly.

A woman on the bench behind shuffled up to make room for me. A man sat down beside the replica Wallaby in front. 'Saved you your seat, mate,' he was told. 'Some bloody Pom tried to take it . . .' Now, either they had just read Austin, or else he had had them in mind when he described the male of the species out here.

The train ride from Circular Quay to Olympic Park via Sydney Central was a dip in a red paintpot. Lions supporters packed the carriages, singing the whole way.

We arrived at Stadium Australia two hours before the game. It was still a magnificent structure sitting in the heart of the Olympic Park, despite the stories that had been doing the rounds since our arrival in Australia that the entire Homebush Bay site was bankrupt. At the time of the Wembley fiasco back in Britain and the collapse of the project to rebuild the stadium in London, Stadium Australia in Sydney had been held up as a shining example of what could be achieved. If there was a collective will, a dynamic vision, a refusal to accept second best etc., etc. . . .

And here, it was, merely ten months after the Olympics, stony, flat broke. Developers had been asked to submit plans for the redevelopment of the redevelopment. One of the problems was that the Homebush Bay Olympic Park, of which Stadium

Australia was the centrepiece, had been built on top of all sorts of polluted industrial sites. And agricultural. There had once been a vast stockyard here, where cattle used to come in by train from all over rural New South Wales to be slaughtered and rendered before being fed to the city. Waste mounds, rising at various intervals around the perimeter, had been covered in topsoil, grass and pretty little flags during the Games, but they contained a lot of nasty chemicals. You had more chance of surviving the nip of a taipan than a dip into the silt beneath the waters of Homebush Bay.

Pollution seemed a common enough problem, but Stadium Australia's difficulties were not quite the same as Britain's. Sydney simply had too many top-quality stadia. The Sydney Football Stadium held 44,000, which was more than enough for any rugby match other than a visit by the All Blacks or the Lions. The All Blacks played in Australia every year in the Tri Nations, but had to be shared around between Brisbane, Sydney and Melbourne. The Lions arrived only once every twelve years. Stadium Australia's 84,000 seats were rarely to be filled. It sat, majestic and empty, fifteen miles from downtown Sydney, leaking money.

But it was magnificent. And on this one night it was going to be full. Not to the 110,000 capacity that had made it bulge on Cathy Freeman nights at the Olympics, or the 107,042 when the All Blacks and Wallabies played to a world-record audience in their Bledisloe Cup match a year before the Games. But 84,188 was not a number to be sneezed at. The Olympic running track had been removed. In its place was being built a lower tier of seats. These were not yet ready, and they sat under the night sky covered in yellow plastic. The empty seats had to support the Wallabies. The vast banks of seats behind the goals, which would come down once the lower redevelopment was completed, rose into the night sky. Up rails built into one of these banks the Olympic torch had travelled, after quite a heart-stopping pause for the Games' organisers and for Cathy Freeman who would light the flame, at the Opening Ceremony. This bank, like its twin at the far end, was now reserved for the Lions supporters. Their seats were open to the elements, and it began to rain, but who cared? The support looked even bigger than ever. I had started my tour groaning at the first fan from Lancashire to harangue me in Townsville, but now the army boomed out a collective optimism that was genuinely uplifting.

The red army was wet. And not even they could hope to monopolise Stadium Australia. But they intended to make their presence felt and let their team know that on this last great stage they would not walk alone.

Meanwhile, down under the overhang of the stands, I was having a beer and a bag of chips. Carbo-stacking before the off. Suddenly a large figure approached. Eddie Butler? Steve Tuynman? Good to see you. And you.

We had played against each other in 1984. He had played number eight in the Grand Slam Wallaby team of that year. I had played in the Welsh team that had been overwhelmed by them and in the Pontypool team that had done rather better and still lost.

Steve was still in rugby, working in coaching and development. It was a bit difficult in New South Wales at that moment because the Union was broke, which rather put the notion of rugby union having the resources to take on rugby league into context. But he had hopes for the future now that Australia had just been promised its fourth franchise in the competition that was to expand from the Super 12 to the Super 14.

It was good to see him. He had been a fine, fine player. We mused on how we had not seen each other for, oh, it must be seventeen years, and yet we could slip easily into small talk. We were hardly going to solve the riddles of the universe, but we were at ease in each other's company. We wondered how many of the current Wallabies and Lions would be able to meet in seventeen years' time and share a soggy chip. God, had they even met socially once on this tour? I suggested that perhaps only Austin Healey and Justin Harrison might be able to sit down one day and have a laugh about what they had been through in

2001. Steve wasn't too sure about that. He was probably right. It may just have been a guilty conscience speaking.

And so, to the final act of the triptych. The pre-match entertainment was on a grand scale. No wonder there was no money in New South Wales rugby. It all went up in smoke and fireworks. The music was stirring. The lower seats glistened like a giant ring of custard. And 'Waltzing Matilda' became 'Waltzing O'Driscoll' once more.

The Lions had managed to turn the despair of Melbourne into hope in Sydney. They were short of their scrum half, who had been imperious throughout the tour, and they were without the wing forward who had proved his world-class worth time and time again. Robert Howley and Richard Hill were absent. But Matt Dawson had filled in for Howley before. Inspirationally so in South Africa, where he had sold the dummy and scored the try that had won the first Test. He was not just a novel diarist, but a proven performer. And Martin Corry had been one of the revelations of the party ever since his arrival from Canada. There had been a strong case for leaving him in the side after the first win in Brisbane. There had been one of those debates, swayed by the benefit of hindsight, that the back row had looked more balanced as Corry, Hill, Quinnell in Brisbane, than as Hill, Back, Quinnell in Melbourne. It was irrelevant now, except that the new Corry, Back, Quinnell formation had only played together once on tour, in the second half in Melbourne, when the game had turned away from the Lions.

There was a casualty counterbalance on the Australians' side. Stephen Larkham and David Giffin were missing. The outside half's shoulder, battered by so many late charges by the Lions' own shoulders, had suffered nerve damage. He had stayed on the field in Melbourne to orchestrate the second-half turnaround, but the price was being paid now. Elton Flatley was in his place. The new hub of the midfield was more physical, more abrupt, but he lacked Larkham's wide-angle vision.

David Giffin had played a large part in upsetting the Lions' line-out in Melbourne. Without set-piece dominance the Lions were never going to win the series. With inconspicuous but effective work, the second row had more than done his bit to bring the series to Sydney all-square. In the week before the decider the Wallabies had been paying attention not so much to the line-out, but the restart kicks. And here they had sought help from another sport. Rodney Eade and Paul Roos, coaches of the Aussie Rules team the Sydney Swans, had offered advice on jumping and catching. Giffin had not taken part. He had paid a price for the Melbourne turnaround, incurring rib damage that allowed Justin Harrison, to win a first cap.

Which side was the more weakened? It was a complicated equation. Howley for Larkham was a fair swap. Hill was probably more important than Giffin, since nullifying George Gregan was an even greater imperative than blunting the Lions' line-out. If Australia had the edge in the fall-out from injury, it was offset by the unexpected presence of Jonny Wilkinson. The medical team had worked their magic. Advantage Lions. Or was there some emotional mileage to be had out of this being Rod Macqueen's last game as coach? The Lions might claim that this was also Graham Henry's last game as Lions coach, but . . . perhaps not.

Justin Harrison – at six feet eight inches reportedly the tallest player in the Australian game – had only started playing rugby at the age of nineteen, when at Southern Cross University in Lismore. Here he was at twenty-seven, winning his first cap on one of the biggest rugby occasions of all time. He had first been called into the Wallaby squad at the end of May, within twenty-four hours of helping the ACT Brumbies beat the Sharks of South Africa and win the Super 12. 'I liken it to finding the fifth gold wrapper to get into Willy Wonka's chocolate factory,' he had said then. He had more in common with Austin than either of them thought.

But was there any substance to the argument that the new cap would be moved to great things as a response to being called a 'plod', a 'plank' and an 'ape' by the diminutive Lion who would not be playing against him? It seemed so. On the Lions' very first throw, the new second row soared above Martin Johnson and won the ball. It led to a penalty which Matt Burke, tonight making his fiftieth appearance for Australia, kicked.

The lead lasted only four minutes. Nathan Grey committed an obstruction, checking Rob Henderson – not with his elbow, it might be added – as the centre put in a little grubber inside the Australian twenty-two. Such an individual ploy by a Lion, by Jeremy Guscott in 1989, had helped win the series. Here, at least, it brought the scores level. Jonny Wilkinson confirmed that all his bones and soft tissue were in working order by kicking his first penalty.

The cycle of the referee awarding a kickable penalty every four minutes continued when Paddy O'Brien of New Zealand judged that Scott Quinnell had not released the ball quickly enough after a tackle made by Andrew Walker. Two out of two for Matt Burke.

And four minutes later another penalty was given. No tit for tat on this occasion, as it was the Lions who were penalised again. It was a worrying penalty at that. The Australians exerted good pressure on a Lions feed at the scrum. Scott Quinnell did well to pick up and make some headway, but after he was tackled the value of George Smith could be seen as the open side arrived quickly and bent down for the ball. This made Quinnell hang on a moment longer than he would have liked. Three out of three for Burke.

Three minutes later the scoring patterns were ruptured on all fronts. A five-metre line-out became a five-metre scrummage. Put-in to the Lions. If they had been discomfited once on their own head, now they drove forward, seeking the pushover try. Australia went backwards, and then down. Penalty try? Paddy O'Brien awarded a re-set scrum. And another, and another.

Finally the ball was released to the Lions backs. Rob Henderson thundered into the tackle. From the ruck, the ball was switched back towards the touchline by Matt Dawson and Jonny Wilkinson. An overlap existed, but the ball would have to travel through the hands of a pair of front-row forwards. As if born to the task, Keith Wood and Tom Smith took the ball, straightened their line of running, swung their hips and moved the ball on. The overlap was perfectly exploited and Jason Robinson crowned his tour with a dash to the corner. For good measure Jonny Wilkinson sent the dreaded Summit ball between the posts from the touchline. The Lions were in the lead 10–9.

Having been insulted by that difficult conversion, the Summit fought back. Both sides were awarded two penalties within kicking range, for a variety of offences. A Lions boot went into a scrum. That was the most heinous. Toutai Kefu collapsed a maul after a line-out and drive threatened to yield a second try for the Lions. Brian O'Driscoll handled the ball on the ground and was perhaps lucky to escape from the bottom of the ruck intact. And there was a simple collective offside. Jonny Wilkinson missed both his shots at goal. As did Matt Burke, although he had the slightest consolation of seeing his first hit the post.

Handling, not kicking, would once again determine the course of the game. Justin Harrison leapt to reclaim a restart. George Gregan then combined with all the backs outside him with the exception of Elton Flatley and Matt Burke. Scrum half fed centre Nathan Grey who fed wing Andrew Walker. Wing to wing, Walker to Joe Roff. And finally to the other centre, Daniel Herbert. The Wallabies could give and take a pass, too. The Lions responded with their most fluent movement of the half, even more flowing than the build-up to the try. They built a multi-phased chain of increasing sophistication as players swapped the position associated with their shirt number for anywhere on the field where they could contribute to the action. Neil Back and Keith Wood, for example, took up the responsibilities of the scrum-half post at least twice each. As the movement cut through, or swayed back and forth across the pitch, the hooter sounded to signal the end of the first half, but only at the next breakdown. The Lions were in no hurry for the half to end. The hooter was new to them, but in Sydney, as in Canberra, they quickly adapted to its bylaws.

The Wallabies were eventually penalised for offside. A penalty did not constitute a break for error or for ball out of play. There was time left for Jonny Wilkinson to kick the points, a slight anti-climax at the end of a sequence containing so much patience, variety and technical expertise. It meant the Lions at the interval were only three points adrift.

In Brisbane as in Melbourne the Tests had been decided in the period immediately following the break. Another common theme was that in neither of those two Tests had the Lions been able to score in the closing quarter. It was strange that they had not been able to score a single point in the closing twenty minutes, when their opponents were at their most exhausted.

First, however, a change had to be made. Scott Quinnell stayed in the changing room, nursing a hamstring strain, and Colin Charvis at last had his chance in a Test. It had no obvious effect on the rhythm of the team. Within three minutes a sliced clearance by Matt Burke had given the Lions a good attacking line-out. They began to string together their phases again. Australia conceded the penalty, but Paddy O'Brien played a good advantage. From a ruck, Jonny Wilkinson, solid of boot, superb as a tackler, suddenly put on his dancing shoes. He indicated to Toutai Kefu he was going on the inside and then slipped past him on the outside to score. He added the conversion, and the Lions were four points in the lead.

Now they needed to stay calm. Colin Charvis decided to throw a quick line-out to himself and run the ball in his own twenty-two. He handed off a couple of defenders and then swung a left boot that skidded the ball along the ground towards touch. It was not exactly the calm consolidation the rest of the team had in mind. They survived the resulting line-out near their line. The danger had passed for the moment.

But then Australia, following a clearance by Rob Henderson, found themselves with another chance to attack from the line-out. Justin Harrison won the ball. On came the drive. Nathan Grey hit the midfield hard and set up a ruck. Toutai Kefu set up another. Daniel Herbert did not have to set up another, for he was over the line for his second try.

The centre's next contribution was the defining moment. He put in a high tackle on Brian O'Driscoll and was sent to the sin-bin. Jonny Wilkinon kicked the penalty. There were still ten minutes to run in the third-quarter period that had decided the

Tests thus far. The scores were now level at 23–all, and the Lions had a one-man advantage.

When Daniel Herbert returned the scores were still level. The Wallabies had held out. There had been a few moments of worry. Rod Moore, for example, had nearly joined Herbert in the sin-bin for stamping at a ruck. The Lions had had two line-out bites five metres out. They had caught and driven and earned themselves one penalty shot at goal. Jonny Wilkinson had missed.

The series hung there at 23–all. With their numbers restored to full strength the Wallabies looked the stronger team. The Lions were having problems on their own throw at the line-out. Graham Henry had always liked the ball thrown long. It was a good way to launch attacks immediately at the heart of the opposition midfield. The Lions had tried it here in an attempt to avoid the competing leaps of John Eales and Justin Harrison. But not with much success.

There was even a whisper that the Wallabies had cracked the Lions' line-out code. Perhaps, in this age of minute attention to detail, it wasn't so improbable. The Lions might, for example, have phoned in the week before the decider to see if they could use the New South Wales training facilities, and one phone call might have led to another, and a little peephole might have opened up. In it, a camera and a directional microphone would have been all that were needed, plus a crossword ace. If the Wallabies had managed it, what an innovating week they had had. Aussie Rules restart specialists and now cryptographers. The Enigma machine won the day.

The Lions, in their own twenty-two, threw long. Perhaps it was the look of alarm on the face of Keith Wood as he planned this launch of the ball. Perhaps it was the sudden set of Martin Corry as he prepared to jump. Perhaps the boosters made the play obvious. Perhaps the code really had been cracked. What-ever the reasons, the long throw was a risk made riskier. There was a lot of moving and shuffling and jostling as the ball took to the air. The Wallabies seemed to jostle the better. Martin Corry had to give a more obvious little shove to have a chance of winning possession. Penalty to Australia. Matt Burke was successful. The Wallabies were three points in front.

More important was their grip on the general management of the game. The Lions basically could not escape their own half of the field. When Colin Charvis again tried to run from deep he was penalised and Matt Burke extended the lead to six points. Half a dozen points. This was what six weeks and two full Tests plus seventy-eight minutes of a third had come down to. Six pox-ridden points. They meant that the Lions needed to score a try and convert it. Just as they had done in Canberra. That game they had won, even after the hooter had sounded. But this was the Test, with so much more at stake. The Wallabies were in control and the final quarter was notorious for not being the Lions' best. They remained stuck in their own half.

And then they escaped. A penalty gave Jonny Wilkinson a chance to push the Lions into the Australian corner. With a kick that he had adapted from Aussie Rules – there were a lot of benefits to be had from the sport – he drilled the Wallabies back.

Now, what would the call be at the line-out? Another long throw? Every Lions supporter prayed not. They prayed that the code was baffling but the throw simple. The target turned out to be the giant himself. Martin Johnson. What else could a captain of his stature do but take responsibility for the biggest line-out of his rugby life? Keith Wood threw, Johnson jumped . . . and Justin Harrison leapt across him and won the ball. It was a sublime moment for the new second row. The plod, the plank. It had been said that he would be stirred up for this one. But if he was thinking about Austin at the very moment of winning the line-out that won the game in the seventy-eighth minute of the deciding Test in front of 84,188 people, then he would surely spend some time in the future in psychotherapy. It was a brilliant moment, but it was merely a reflection of his consummate rugby skills.

The Lions had two more chances from the line-out. Neither was in immediate striking range of the try line. They threw to Danny Grewcock in the middle but were soon turned over in the centre of the field. They threw long to Martin Corry and developed a move that was heading for the far corner until the Australians scrambled the ball into touch. The hooter had already sounded the game was over. The Wallabies had beaten the Lions for the first time ever in a series. The world champions had triumphed again, adding the scalp of the British and Irish Lions to the World Cup, the Bledisloe Cup and the Tri Nations title they held. For John Eales, as he collected the Tom Richards Cup and raised it before the biggest crowd ever to witness a Lions game, it was the crowning glory to a wonderful playing career. Rod Macqueen could take his leave now, saying that there was nothing left to win in the game.

For the Lions there was nothing, full stop.

I wondered what I should do about Austin. Half-heartedly I tried his mobile a couple of times. No reply. And then he answered. 'Are you OK?' I asked. 'Yes, OK,' he replied. I paused and he paused.

'Where do you want to do it?' he asked. On a tour full of secretiveness and misinformation, Austin was a model of straightforwardness.

I told him I'd meet him outside the entrance to the tunnel. As I neared the door to the changing-room area, I saw Austin take a step back and duck. I must admit, I did the same, tucking myself behind a door. Donal Lenihan, Graham Henry and Alex Broun swept past, on their way to the press conference.

Austin was outstanding as always. He wanted to know if the *Guardian* and *Observer* would pay his fine. He said it looked as if they were going to haul him up before some Star Chamber. I said I'd do my best to organise it. He paid tribute to the lads who'd given it their all. He congratulated Justin Harrison who had played very well. 'Fair play to him.' He said Donal Lenihan had addressed the whole squad in the changing room after the game. 'We all knew where Donal was coming from,' he said. 'There were a few tears. We all clapped at the end.' Graham Henry had then spoken to the Lions. 'And?' I asked. 'And nothing,' said Austin. 'Silence.'

15

Aftermath

The next morning at eleven o'clock Graham Henry gave his final briefing. Any notion – any hope – that he might climb out of bed with a hangover, turn up and thrash things out with unrestrained fury, sadness, indignation, resignation or whatever, vanished when he ignored the first question and told us that he had been for a walk along the Manly Promenade, had a swim and would now like to make a statement.

There was obviously huge disappointment, he stated, that the series had been lost. But it had been a close-run thing in the backyard of the world champions. The standard of play had been very high on both sides, and the two teams had been separated in the end by six points. The real chance had come in Melbourne. After that it had been a struggle to put fifteen guys on the field. Australia were going to be at their best in Sydney, and the Lions had been struggling to put half a side together on the training paddock in the build-up, let alone field a team in prime condition on the big night.

That was fair enough, although I was reminded of his words to me as we walked back to the hotel: 'If the Wallabies play well and we play well, we'll win.' But it had only been a fleeting chat, after all.

He was right about the standard of play. The series was destined to be a gruelling slog decided by the odd kick, we had assumed at the outset. It had turned out to be a running series of thrillers where Jason Robinson and Brian O'Driscoll could blossom, where Jonny Wilkinson was an all-round master rather than a specialist kicker.

But then Graham Henry changed tack. He talked of his methods and of the future. The game had changed. It had been necessary to train the way they had, to freeze the cultural experience as they had, because it was a professional game now. In Perth he had said that there was a missionary value to the Lions. He was not so sure now. The case would have to be made for bringing a smaller squad and for playing Saturday games only. The schedule might comprise little more than a couple of warm-up games and a Test series. It was a dispiriting end to his time in charge. Far from being a defender of the Lions tradition, Graham Henry was now seeking to dismantle it.

Unfortunately, he had opted for a management style that left him on the outside of the ways of the rugby player, ancient or modern, of Britain and Ireland. The midweek team that he now wished to abandon had already been abandoned. By him. They had been left to prepare themselves on a Monday – if they were allowed even that time – for their big day on a Tuesday. And they had lost only once, in a close encounter against a fine Australia A team. The game against ACT Brumbies had been a classic of its kind. The dirt-trackers had done themselves proud, and now their non-coach wanted them to stay at home in future.

The Test team on which he had spent all his time and analytical powers had lost twice and had not had the energy to score a single point in the closing stages of any Test. For all the holistics thrown their way, they looked spent at times when the Wallabies were still going strong.

Perhaps he was thinking of numbers, of having too many inactive players wandering around with little to do other than grow ripe for sedition. He said he was amazed at what Austin Healey had said before the final Test. It was ammunition for the enemy. At the start of the tour the Lions had apparently come together to take some sacred oath that, however tough it became in Australia, they would not vent their frustrations in public. Well, how many of the Lions, on solemnly taking their pledge of silence, had ever thought that the object of their simmering resentment would be the internal politics of the tour? They could take the Aussie grief, but why suffer in silence when their supposed experience of a lifetime turned out to be utter hell?

Nobody, of course, had been more outspoken than Austin. But who represented the real spirit of the Lions? Graham Henry, cold, distant, secretive, repressive and – heaven forbid – without knowledge of the word punctual? Or Austin Healey, impish, troublesome, gobby, chippy, outspoken, heroic on the field, proud to be English and a Lion, and, last but not least, on time?

The Lions tour failed, but only just, as a rugby adventure. That was bad enough for the most treasured people in the game, the players. As a human experience it was not so much a miserable failure for them, as just plain miserable. That was no way to travel the world, even as a professional. When Graham Henry had finished trying to put as much blame as possible on Austin Healey, the Lions party broke up and in a somewhat fractured and anti-climactic way we drifted out of sunny Manly and began to travel the world again, on the long journey home.

Austin had already left for Hawaii. He was off first thing on the Sunday morning. His wife Louise and he left, with Martin and Kay Johnson, for a break: beach and sun, and with mobile phones turned off.

I hoped their departure had been so early that they would not have had time to read the Sunday papers. He was chased out of Australia by headlines of good riddance. How had Australian Customs ever let him in the first place, Simon Poidevin, the ex-Wallaby wing forward and now television co-commentator, wanted to know?

A paper chase began back home in Britain. Newspaper after newspaper gave Austin stick. He was daft, he had lost the Lions the series, he was responsible for global warming. Ian Wooldridge in the *Daily Mail* was particularly harsh, not so much on Austin as a greenhouse gas, but as foolish and, dash it, nigh on treacherous.

I wrote a piece in the *Observer* saying that I was Austin.
Which was a bit of a moment in my life, I must say. Not exactly
Austin, but Austin's ghost-writer. He had given me the low-
down on the tour, and I had said I would not land him in trouble.
I emphasised that not once had he ever criticised a Lions player.
There had been a trickle of criticism at the coaches throughout,
but never the players. Australia, yes. And one Australian in
particular – Justin Harrison.

The development of their feud in print had been my doing. I
had found it intriguing that the biggest player in Australian
rugby and one of the smallest Lions should have engaged in an
ongoing spat that would only be resolved on the big stage when
they were both called up for the Teams for the showdown finale.
Except, of course, that the story never reached its conclusion.
Austin missed the Test thanks to his bulging disc. He left for
Hawaii branded a blight on Australia.

He had been heroic on the field, and was one of the very few
players to break down the preconception that the Test team had
been picked before any of the party ever set foot in Australia. His
performances in the midweek team had 'sparked us' – and those
were Graham Henry's words. He played his way into the Test
team. He might have been impish to the point of irritating in the
eyes of his fellow players at times, but he had made a lasting – no
doubt about that – contribution. A Lions tour was a warm-
hearted, emotional, passionate affair, I wrote at my most flowery.
Graham Henry had brought to it the warmth of a North Sea cod.

I phoned Austin two weeks after the tour ended, He was just
back from Hawaii and was pushing a trolley around a supermarket in Leicester. 'Anything been happening?' he asked. I told
him he had been red-hot news. 'I thought something must have
been happening,' he said. 'I picked up a load of hate mail at the
club this morning. Very interesting.'

'How do you feel about that?' I asked.

'Well, it's all calmed down now,' he said. 'It'll brew back up, I
should think, around the time of the disciplinary meeting. I'll
give you a ring then.'

He didn't ask me why I had written the final blast. I had said I wouldn't drop him in it, and I had. Why? Four reasons, I think. Bear with me. I recognise that it's self-indulgent, but this is a bit of a confessional.

First, the fact that I had spiked the mutiny story, the one Austin told me in Brisbane ten days before the Matt Dawson diary, rankled a bit. I didn't mind altering the original column, in order not to place Austin on the rack, but there were other ways to disclose the serious internal dissent. It was a good story and it slipped away.

Second, the phone call from Alex Broun at 1.30 in the morning after the Melbourne Test. Could I show him Austin's column? No. Could I read it to him, then? It was absurd, suddenly being part of some letter-reading censorship. Sorry, we'll have to put a black line through that sentence . . . and that one. And just as absurd was disobediently inventing a few lines as I obediently dictated it down the phone, to make it blander yet. The tour management wanted control over what was written. If I told the *Observer* that I was part of a propaganda machine that was only going to produce complimentary pieces, they would wish me all the best in my career in public relations and find themselves somebody new on the rugby beat.

Third, what was wrong with Austin winding up Australia with a few choice remarks about its male population? It wasn't politically correct, it wasn't clever-witty, but rugby players on the eve of an international match are not politically correct, ha-ha funny beasts. They sway wildly between rushes of adrenaline and bouts on the physiotherapist's table. Elation is mixed with nervousness, the desire to get stuck right in tempered by the race to get the body in some sort of shape to survive its ordeal.

Fourth, I had written Austin's column and then gone out to dinner at Doyle's on the Beach in Watsons Bay. I hadn't filed the column earlier because, after the muting of the mutiny, I was in the habit of checking it. Just to see that what I had committed to paper in the first flush of being Austin would pass inspection. Well, this time, when I returned, I didn't bother. Off it went with a few presses of the keyboard, full of its planks and plods. Sorry, Justin. Sorry, Austin.

In future, the rules about ghosted columns would change. The wish among the journalists was that the codes of practice imposed by the governing bodies would be so tight that the player as columnist ceased to exist. One amanuensis among us had to have his work inspected by a player's father before it was approved for publication. Having dropped Austin in it I could see this particular dad's point, but I'd prefer to go down the line of freedom of speech rather than parental guidance. No, I'd rather have material that made for a half-decent read over a cup of coffee than have a father from hell act as sub-editor. The whole sports-column business, as written by players, lay at the silly end of the industry. Well, it did for the ghost-writers.

Before the tour I was only asked once for the record what I thought the outcome of the series would be. I think it was by a bloke from Ceefax. I said 2–1 to the Wallabies. During the tour, I changed my mind. This was a Lions outfit that should have won the Test series. Not easily, but by a margin that expressed a discernible superiority. Rod Macqueen always said that the Lions would be the best rugby side ever to visit Australian shores.

They weren't. They should have been, but they weren't. With their large quota of outstanding English players supplemented by the best of the rest – and of those, Rob Howley, Brian O'Driscoll and Keith Wood were world-class on tour – the firepower was there to make this the best team in the world. By definition in this age of rapid improvement, that meant the best side the world had seen.

Graham Henry was perhaps right to tone down the unbridled expansiveness of the new English game. Setting the Six Nations alight and making Twickenham a temple of adventure were not the same as playing in Australia against the world champions, who were blessed with levels of fitness second to none. But the process of strategic refinement had to be sensitively handled. Iain Balshaw was the casualty of a system that told him to run hard into midfield. The sensation of the Six Nations, who liked to run any which way to avoid the tackle, was not designed for crash-ball charging. It was no wonder his form and confidence plummeted. Was the situation ever explained to him in terms that made him feel still valued?

Injuries played their part. The toll was at its highest in the early stages of the tour, during the days of double sessions of training and of uncertainty on the field as players were feeling their way down the path to becoming an assured collective. Such fatigue and such uncertainty were a sure way to leave players lying down. Crocked tourists were replaced and Martin Corry turned out to be one hell of a substitute. He had a history of being overlooked – as he had been again when the original touring party was selected – but he was the converse of Iain Balshaw. So little was expected and so much was delivered.

Richard Hill, whom Martin replaced for the final Test, was, however, sorely missed. Michael Jones of New Zealand, around the time of the 1987 World Cup, took the standards of back-row play to a new high. He was conspicuous in every single aspect of play, except for anything happening on a Sunday. Jones thought that Sundays were for church and not for chasing a pig's bladder. Sundays were Sundays to Richard Hill. Like Mondays were Mondays. Days were just days. Any day was for rugby. He was not conspicuous. But he was just as revolutionary in performance as Michael Jones. He had that priceless gift of being able to do his job to perfection. Had he been fit the result might have been different in Sydney.

Would the Lions have thrown long at the line-out so often in the final Test if Hill had been fit? Corry was taller, a more natural target. If Hill had been playing, might Danny Grewcock have been used more? Then again, Graham Henry liked long ball and had worked out a theory, based on what he did best – poring over video after video – that long was a tactic that might work. It did not. The Wallabies had done their homework even better. They nullified the Lions' jumpers.

The Australian scrummage, moreover, was stronger than it was supposed to be. Rod Moore came into the front row after the Brisbane Test and did the job of preventing the Lions from tying the Wallabies down to heavyweight set-piece work. Did he turn in and under? He was not penalised, and that was all that counted.

The Wallabies tightened up the defence that had leaked so copiously in Brisbane. They plugged the gaps through which Rob Henderson ran in the first Test. And as far as it was possible to keep a lid on Brian O'Driscoll, they did just that. Nathan Grey made the tackle of the series on the Lions' star. Rod Macqueen won the personal duel of the coaches.

And, facing the cliff-face of green-and-gold support at Stadium Australia, Justin Harrison won his one big personal line-out against Martin Johnson. At the end of the game, when the series hung in the balance, the captain of the Lions took responsibility for the call. He would be the target. He would catch the ball the forwards would drive in low, their legs would take the short pumping steps that would drive the maul towards the line. Neil Back would steer the human contraption and would score the try. Right in the corner. It would not matter. Jonny Wilkinson would place the Summit ball down, tight against the sideline, twenty-five metres back from the tryline. He would hold his hands, as if he were cupping a sparrow that had flown into the kitchen, and would then step up and send the ball clean over for the conversion to win the series. It would have been the sequence to end all sequences.

But Justin Harrison won the line-out. The new cap took the ball off the Lions' totem. It was the piece of cheek to end all pieces of cheek. Of course, if Austin had been there, it would have been different. By the seventy-eighth minute both second row and wing would have been in the sin-bin. Or the early bath, or hospital, or prison. Dangling like Bob and Jack at the end of a rope, Austin with his tongue out and Justin with his toes scraping the ground, still trying to flick out a knee.

The tour would not be remembered as a fantasy. It would not be remembered for the reality of being a near-miss. Lions tours that had gone down bravely in the Test series were fairly commonplace. What set this tour apart and made it unforgettable was its corrosive, even explosive, human chemistry.

So many noble words had been composed in Hampshire by professional people, so that a professional rugby team might beat the clock and come together, bonded by mutual respect and a shared vision, to be the best to beat the best. The mission statement. The credo of team spirit on the field, off the field was, as always, the obsession. Fifty hearts had to beat as one, remember?

Why? Rugby is a game designed to suit all shapes and sizes. If it was deemed a speciality of the sport to cater for people of varying bodily shapes, why not accommodate differences of mind as well? Playing a silly game together, all being in harmony on the field, singing from the same hymn-sheet for the duration of a game, was one thing. But rugby has a terrible tradition of trying to control the thoughts of the collective. Codes of practice, rules of communication, mission statements. My arse.

The old saying that 'what happened on tour stayed on tour' was exactly that, an old saying. It was both of a time of serious fornication and even more serious wreckage to property while the lads were away from home for a long time. It was the *omerta* of shamateurism. It was the only titbit from the old age that became cherished in the new – and it was as out of place as travelling to Australia by steamship.

All those platitudes about respect, dignity, honesty, mutual support; all these fine words were supposed to be, I imagine, a comfort blanket. Something for which you reached when things became a little hairy. But once the blanket had been presented at the corporate seminar in Hampshire, it was hung up like a piece of granny's needlework. Nice, but serving no real purpose. So it was stuck up who knew where . . . over there, out of the way.

And, with the pretty words out of the way, all the separate agendas could begin. The analysts went off to analyse and the trainers to train, the players to play. Except that some of them didn't think they were given a chance. The shared vision was immediately blurred. The mutual respect and the oath of candour and honesty did not survive the first week. By the time the

Lions reached Brisbane first time round, ten days into the tour, the comfort blanket was torn down and waved as a flag of revolt.

Steve Black would say that he was not worried by the disaffection of the players. He would have been amazed if international players, accustomed to being automatic first-choice for their country, did not feel resentful at being overlooked for Test selection. Anything beyond private frustration was intolerable, however, in his book. Players had to realise what was hard in life and what was not. Shift-workers in a factory and miners underground had a hard life. Going out onto a rugby field and organising the line-out did not constitute having a hard time. The players had to be a bit tougher mentally than that. They were living out a lot of people's fantasies.

Exactly. People didn't travel to Australia in their tens of thousands to watch anthracite being hewn. The players were aware of the privileged position their particular skills warranted them in life. Nobody had become a Lion by being a shirker. There was no comparison between everyday life and the life of a British and Irish Lion. Besides, the musings on hardship were from the man who was supposed to be giving out the spoonful of sugar to help down the medicine of training and playing in a fractious environment. Ronan O'Gara was no doubt comforted by Steve Black's holistic homilies. If the spiritual counsellor thought the grumblers – not that the Irish out-half was one – were wimps, think what the real slave-drivers in the management team thought of mutiny. Malcolm O'Kelly was not a mutineer. He was bright, witty, underplayed and unhappy on tour. Steve Black said it was not a boot camp. Malcolm O'Kelly recorded on tape: 'It does feel like being in the army.'

Steve Black said, as far back as Tylney Hall, that the Lions had not socialised much, but that this might be no bad thing. It helped focus the mind on the job. Malcolm O'Kelly thought that 'Not enough was being done socially. You needed a release, to let the madness out.'

The tenor of the tour was austere. Martin Johnson was never going to adhere to any ethos other than one bathed in sweat. His

Test team went with him. He had been through this before, as had his senior lieutenants. To be the best you had to work harder than the best. They were disciples of a Spartan school of thought. They went across Australia and travelled up and down it without seeing it. A vast land of magical variety was condensed into one rugby field after another. One stadium led to the next. They saw videos of rugby, they prowled hotel rooms and they sat at team meetings. This was not a Lions tour; it was a business trip. And Steve Black said it wasn't even hard.

The frosty trip to a country of sunshine could have been salvaged only by victory. And on that score the Lions tour failed to deliver as well. It was close enough to be agonising. Except, of course, the Lions of 2001 didn't do agonising. It was probably unsatisfactory. All the fine words had been put away.

It was perhaps for the best. The guinea-pig experiment in professional touring came within a converted try of success. The regime offered a template of how tours might be conducted in future. Mercifully, this template could now be melted down.

The Lions visit to New Zealand in 2005 would have to be approached from a fresh stance. There would be a rugby-mad country to tour, of course, one whose approach might register as middling-to-toughish on the 2001 scale of duress. But there would also be a chance to acknowledge, at the very least, that a nation on the other side of the globe was holding out a hand of welcome. Rugby was not the only thing to analyse on a Lions tour. The future of the adventure would have to look back to a mould shaped deeper in the past than the model offered by Graham Henry and the tangled tour of 2001.

Index